THE BIG BOO
LOW CARB DIET

1500 Days Of Delicious No-Sugar Added Recipes To Forget About Carb Counting Yet Living a Fulfilling Low-Carb Lifestyle. 28-Day Meal Plan Included

JUDITH C. JONES

EDITOR: LYN   INTERIOR DESIGN: FAIZAN

COVER ART: ABR   FOOD STYLIST: JO

LOW CARBOHYDRATE DIET

Table of Contents

Introduction

Welcome to the fascinating world of low carb dieting—a realm of delicious possibilities, transformative health benefits, and a fresh perspective on how we approach nutrition.

In recent years, the concept of low carb diets has gained significant attention, sparking discussions and debates within the realm of nutrition. As we delve deeper into the intricacies of carbohydrates and their impact on our bodies, we begin to understand the profound influence they have on our well-being. Low carb diets offer an alternative approach to eating—one that challenges traditional beliefs and paves the way for a new understanding of nutrition.

In the following pages, you will embark on a journey of knowledge, discovery, and practical application. Our aim is to equip you with the tools and insights necessary to make informed choices about your dietary habits and embrace the power of low carb living. Here, we strive to demystify the complexities of macronutrients, debunk common myths, and empower you with the knowledge to take charge of your health.

Within these chapters, you will find a wealth of resources, including detailed explanations of the science behind low carb diets, the metabolic processes involved, and the potential benefits they can offer. We'll explore the role of carbohydrates in our bodies, the impact of insulin, and the intricate dance between food and our overall well-being. But more importantly, we will guide you through the practical aspects of adopting a low carb lifestyle—meal planning, grocery shopping, and mastering the art of preparing delectable, low carb meals.

However, it is crucial to recognize that every individual is unique, and there is no one-size-fits-all approach to nutrition. What works for one person may not yield the same results for another. Our intention is not to advocate for rigid dietary rules, but rather to provide you with the knowledge and flexibility to make informed choices that align with your specific needs and goals.

As you embark on this journey, remember that balance and moderation are key. Low carb living is not about complete elimination or deprivation; rather, it encourages a mindful and intentional approach to food. It invites us to appreciate the abundance of nutrient-dense whole foods and to savor the flavors and textures they offer.

Whether you seek weight management, blood sugar control, improved energy levels, or simply a greater sense of vitality, low carb diets can serve as a powerful tool on your path to better health. But remember, health is not just about what we eat—it encompasses a holistic approach that encompasses movement, stress management, and self-care.

Chapter 1
Understanding Low Carb Diets

The Principles of Low Carb Living

The principles of low carb living revolve around reducing the intake of carbohydrates while focusing on consuming adequate protein, healthy fats, and nutrient-dense foods. Here are the key principles in detail:

LIMIT CARBOHYDRATE INTAKE

The primary principle of a low carb diet is to limit the consumption of carbohydrates. This typically involves reducing or avoiding high-carb foods such as refined grains, sugary foods and beverages, and starchy vegetables. Instead, the emphasis is on choosing carbohydrates from whole, unprocessed sources such as non-starchy vegetables, nuts, seeds, and low-sugar fruits.

FOCUS ON NUTRIENT-DENSE FOODS

Low carb living encourages a focus on nutrient-dense foods that provide essential vitamins, minerals, and antioxidants. This includes incorporating plenty of non-starchy vegetables like leafy greens, cruciferous vegetables, and colorful varieties. These vegetables are low in carbs, high in fiber, and offer a wide range of health-promoting compounds.

PRIORITIZE PROTEIN

Protein plays a crucial role in low carb diets as it helps promote satiety, preserve muscle mass, and support various bodily functions. Including adequate protein sources like lean meats, poultry, fish, eggs, tofu, tempeh, and legumes helps meet nutrient needs and maintain a feeling of fullness.

EMBRACE HEALTHY FATS

Low carb living encourages the consumption of healthy fats to provide energy and promote satiety. Sources of healthy fats include avocados, nuts and seeds, olive oil, coconut oil, fatty fish like salmon and sardines, and grass-fed butter. These fats provide essential fatty acids and fat-soluble vitamins.

Minimize Processed and Sugary Foods: Low carb diets often involve reducing or eliminating highly processed foods and foods high in added sugars. Processed foods tend to be high in refined carbohydrates, unhealthy fats, and additives. By avoiding or minimizing these foods, low carb living promotes a more whole-food, nutrient-dense approach to eating.

INDIVIDUALIZE CARBOHYDRATE INTAKE

Low carb diets recognize that carbohydrate needs can vary among individuals based on factors such as activity level, metabolic health, and personal goals. Some people may benefit from a very low carb or ketogenic approach (typically under 50 grams of carbs per day), while others may find success with a moderate carb intake (around 50-100 grams per day). Individualizing carbohydrate intake allows for flexibility and customization.

MINDFUL EATING AND PORTION CONTROL

Low carb living emphasizes mindful eating and paying attention to hunger and fullness cues. It encourages portion control to avoid excessive calorie intake, even with low carb foods. Being mindful of food choices, eating slowly, and savoring the flavors can help foster a healthier relationship with food.

The Benefits of Low Carb Living

WEIGHT MANAGEMENT AND ITS CONNECTION TO LOW CARB DIETS

i. Enhanced Fat Burning: Low carb diets can promote weight loss by stimulating the body to burn stored fat for energy. By reducing carbohydrate intake, insulin levels decrease, allowing the body to access fat stores more readily. This metabolic shift promotes fat burning and can lead to weight loss.

ii. Satiety and Reduced Calorie Intake: Low carb diets are often associated with increased feelings of satiety and reduced hunger. Protein and healthy fats, which are staples of low carb diets, tend to be more filling and can help control appetite. As a result, individuals may naturally consume fewer calories, aiding in weight management.

iii. Decreased Cravings and Emotional Eating: Low carb diets may help reduce cravings for sugary and high-carb foods. By stabilizing blood sugar levels and avoiding rapid spikes and crashes, individuals are less likely to experience intense cravings and are better able to control emotional eating patterns.

Blood sugar control and the benefits for individuals with diabetes or insulin resistance

i. Improved Insulin Sensitivity: Low carb diets have been shown to improve insulin sensitivity, allowing the body to utilize insulin more efficiently. This can be especially beneficial for individuals with diabetes or insulin resistance, as it helps regulate blood sugar levels and reduce the need for exogenous insulin or other diabetes medications.

ii. Stable Blood Sugar Levels: By limiting carbohydrate intake, low carb diets help prevent rapid blood sugar spikes and promote more stable blood sugar levels throughout the day. This can reduce the risk of hyperglycemia and support better overall glycemic control.

APPETITE CONTROL AND THE ROLE OF STABLE BLOOD SUGAR LEVELS

i. Reduced Hunger and Increased Satiety: Low carb diets, particularly those higher in protein and healthy fats, can help regulate appetite and promote a feeling of fullness. Stable blood sugar levels achieved through low carb eating contribute to balanced hunger hormones, reducing excessive hunger and cravings.

ii. Better Control Over Portion Sizes: Low carb diets, when combined with mindful eating practices, can help individuals develop better portion control habits. By focusing on nutrient-dense, satiating foods, individuals are more likely to consume appropriate portion sizes and avoid overeating.

EXPLORING POTENTIAL BENEFITS FOR HEART HEALTH

i. Improved Blood Lipid Profile: Low carb diets have been associated with improvements in blood lipid profile, including decreased levels of triglycerides and increased levels of HDL (good) cholesterol. These changes may contribute to a reduced risk of heart disease.

ii. Reduced Inflammation: Some studies suggest that low carb diets can help reduce markers of inflammation, such as C-reactive protein (CRP). Chronic inflammation is a known risk factor for heart disease, and reducing inflammation can support better heart health.

iii. Weight Loss and Metabolic Health: Low carb diets can contribute to weight loss and improvements in metabolic markers such as blood pressure, blood sugar control, and insulin sensitivity. These factors play a crucial role in maintaining a healthy cardiovascular system.

Frequently Asked Questions

WHAT FOODS SHOULD I EAT ON A LOW-CARB DIET?

On a low-carb diet, the focus is on reducing carbohydrate intake while emphasizing protein, healthy fats, and non-starchy vegetables. Here's a breakdown of the foods you should eat on a low-carb diet:

PROTEIN SOURCES
Include lean meats such as chicken, turkey, beef, and pork. Opt for skinless poultry and lean cuts of red meat. Fish and seafood are excellent choices as they are low in carbs and high in healthy fats. Eggs are also a great source of protein.

HEALTHY FATS
Incorporate healthy fats into your low-carb diet. Avocados are rich in monounsaturated fats and fiber. Nuts and seeds like almonds, walnuts, chia seeds, and flaxseeds provide healthy fats and essential nutrients. Olive oil, coconut oil, and avocado oil are good options for cooking and dressings.

NON-STARCHY VEGETABLES
Non-starchy vegetables are low in carbs and packed with essential nutrients and fiber. Include leafy greens like spinach, kale, and lettuce. Other options include broccoli, cauliflower, zucchini, bell peppers, cucumbers, and mushrooms. These vegetables can be eaten raw, steamed, sautéed, or incorporated into salads or stir-fries.

DAIRY PRODUCTS
Dairy products can be consumed in moderation, depending on individual tolerance. Opt for full-fat or low-fat options like Greek yogurt, cottage cheese, and hard cheeses. These provide protein and calcium but be mindful of added sugars in flavored varieties.

BERRIES
Berries such as strawberries, blueberries, raspberries, and blackberries are lower in carbs compared to other fruits. They can be enjoyed in moderation due to their antioxidant content and relatively low glycemic impact.

LEGUMES

Legumes like lentils, chickpeas, and black beans can be included in moderation, especially for individuals who tolerate them well. They provide a good source of plant-based protein and fiber.

BEVERAGES

Water should be the primary beverage on a low-carb diet. It's important to stay hydrated throughout the day. Unsweetened tea, coffee, and herbal infusions are also suitable choices. Limit or avoid sugary beverages, fruit juices, and alcoholic drinks high in carbs.

ARE ALL CARBOHYDRATES OFF-LIMITS ON A LOW-CARB DIET?

Not all carbohydrates are off-limits on a low-carb diet. While the emphasis is on reducing carb intake, it's important to differentiate between "good" and "bad" carbs. Here's a breakdown of carbohydrate sources and their role in a low-carb diet:

AVOID REFINED AND PROCESSED CARBS

Refined grains like white bread, pasta, and white rice, as well as sugary foods and processed snacks, should be limited or avoided on a low-carb diet. These foods are typically high in refined carbohydrates and have a high glycemic index, which can spike blood sugar levels and lead to cravings and energy crashes.

CHOOSE NUTRIENT-DENSE CARBOHYDRATES

Not all carbohydrates are created equal. Nutrient-dense carbohydrates should be chosen over empty-calorie options. Focus on carbohydrates that are high in fiber, vitamins, and minerals. Examples include non-starchy vegetables like leafy greens, broccoli, cauliflower, asparagus, and bell peppers.

MODERATE FRUIT CONSUMPTION

Fruits contain natural sugars and varying amounts of fiber. While some fruits are higher in carbs, they can still be enjoyed in moderation. Berries, such as strawberries, blueberries, and raspberries, tend to be lower in carbs compared to tropical fruits. Be mindful of portion sizes and aim for whole fruits rather than juices.

CHOOSE WHOLE GRAINS WISELY

If you decide to include grains, choose whole grains that are higher in fiber and have a lower impact on blood sugar levels. Examples include quinoa, buckwheat, brown rice, and oats. Portion control is important, as even whole grains contain carbohydrates that can add up quickly.

CONSIDER LEGUMES

Legumes like lentils, chickpeas, and black beans are higher in carbohydrates but also provide a good source of fiber, protein, and other nutrients. They can be included in moderate amounts, depending on individual tolerance.

HOW MANY CARBS SHOULD I EAT ON A LOW-CARB DIET?

The number of carbs you should consume on a low-carb diet can vary depending on individual factors such as activity level, metabolic health, and weight loss goals. Here are some general guidelines to consider:

KETOGENIC APPROACH

A strict ketogenic diet typically limits carbohydrate intake to around 20-50 grams per day. This very low-carb approach aims to induce ketosis, a metabolic state in which the body primarily uses fat for fuel.

LOW-CARB RANGE

For most people following a low-carb diet, a range of 50-100 grams of net carbs per day is commonly recommended. Net carbs are calculated by subtracting fiber from the total carbohydrate content of a food.

PERSONALIZATION

It's important to customize your carbohydrate intake based on your individual needs and goals. Factors like age, gender, activity level, and metabolic health can influence the ideal carb range for you. Some individuals may need to stay at the lower end of the range to achieve desired results, while others may be able to tolerate slightly higher carb intake.

TRIAL AND ERROR

Finding your optimal carb intake may involve some trial and error. Gradually reducing carbohydrate intake while monitoring your body's response can help you determine the right balance. Pay attention to energy levels, satiety, weight loss progress, and overall well-being.

QUALITY OF CARBS

While counting grams of carbs is important, it's equally crucial to focus on the quality of carbs consumed. Prioritize nutrient-dense, whole food sources of carbohydrates like vegetables, nuts, seeds, and berries, rather than relying on processed or refined carbohydrate sources.

INDIVIDUALIZATION

It's essential to individualize your carb intake based on your health goals, lifestyle, and preferences. Some people may find that they perform better with slightly higher carb intake, especially if they engage in intense physical activity or have specific dietary needs.

IS A LOW-CARB DIET SAFE FOR EVERYONE?

In general, a low-carb diet is considered safe for most healthy individuals. However, it's important to note that individual responses may vary, and certain populations may require modifications or additional considerations. Here are some factors to keep in mind regarding the safety of a low-carb diet:

UNDERLYING HEALTH CONDITIONS

If you have any underlying health conditions or concerns, it's crucial to consult with a healthcare professional before making significant dietary changes. Conditions such as diabetes, kidney disease, liver disease, or a history of eating disorders may require specific adjustments to ensure safety and optimal health.

MEDICATIONS

Certain medications, such as those for diabetes or high blood pressure, may need to be adjusted when following a low-carb diet. It's essential to work closely with your healthcare provider to monitor and manage any necessary medication modifications.

NUTRIENT ADEQUACY

While a low-carb diet can be nutritionally balanced, it's important to ensure that you're obtaining adequate nutrients. Focus on consuming a variety of nutrient-dense foods, including non-starchy vegetables, healthy fats, and high-quality sources of protein. Consider working with a registered dietitian to help optimize nutrient intake and avoid any potential deficiencies.

INDIVIDUALIZED APPROACH

A low-carb diet may need to be customized based on individual needs and preferences. For example, athletes or individuals with high physical activity levels may require slightly higher carbohydrate intake to support performance and recovery. Pregnant or breastfeeding women may also have different nutritional requirements.

LONG-TERM SUSTAINABILITY

While a low-carb diet can be safe in the short term, it's important to consider long-term sustainability and overall dietary balance. It's advisable to focus on incorporating a wide variety of nutrient-rich foods, including fruits, vegetables, whole grains, and legumes, when appropriate.

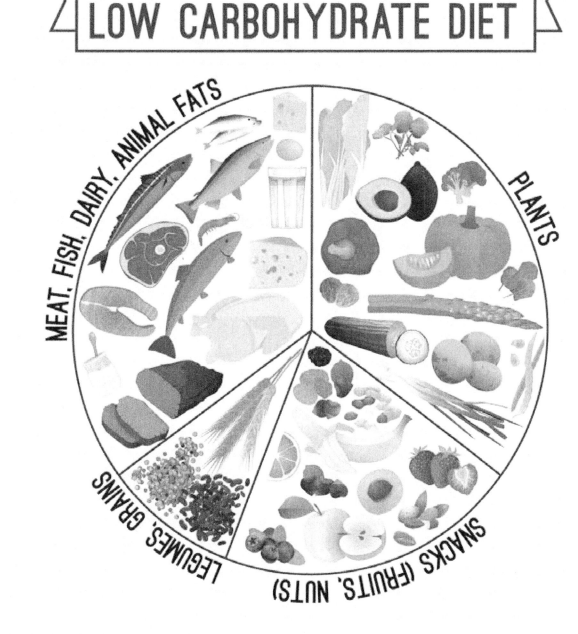

Start Without Guesswork

A. FINDING BALANCE AND SUSTAINABILITY IN LOW CARB DIETS:

i. Long-Term Approach: Low carb diets are most effective when approached as a long-term lifestyle change rather than a short-term solution. Focus on finding a balance that works for you and is sustainable in the long run. This might involve experimenting with different levels of carb intake, incorporating occasional indulgences, and allowing flexibility within your dietary choices.

ii. Listening to Your Body: Pay attention to how your body responds to different levels of carbohydrate intake. Some individuals may thrive on a very low carb or ketogenic approach, while others may find a moderate carb intake more sustainable. Tune in to your body's cues and adjust your carbohydrate intake accordingly to find the right balance that supports your energy levels, performance, and overall well-being.

B. ADAPTING LOW CARB EATING TO INDIVIDUAL NEEDS AND PREFERENCES:

i. Personalization: Low carb diets can be adapted to individual needs, preferences, and dietary restrictions. Whether you follow a vegetarian, vegan, or gluten-free diet, there are plenty of low carb options available. Focus on incorporating nutrient-dense, low carb foods that align with your dietary preferences to ensure enjoyment and adherence.

ii. Individualized Carb Intake: Recognize that carbohydrate needs may vary among individuals based on factors such as activity level, metabolism, and health goals. Experiment with different levels of carbohydrate intake and assess how your body responds. Gradually adjust your carb intake to find the sweet spot that provides the desired benefits while supporting your individual needs.

C. EXPLORING INGREDIENT VARIETY AND SUBSTITUTIONS:

i. Ingredient Variety: Low carb diets offer a wide range of ingredients to explore and enjoy. Embrace the variety of non-starchy vegetables, proteins, healthy fats, and low-sugar fruits available. Experiment with different flavors, textures, and cooking methods to keep your meals interesting and satisfying.

ii. Substitutions: Low carb living often involves finding creative substitutions for high-carb ingredients. Explore alternatives such as using cauliflower rice instead of regular rice, lettuce wraps instead of tortillas, or spiralized vegetables in place of pasta. Discovering low carb substitutions allows you to still enjoy your favorite dishes while maintaining your dietary goals.

D. ADDRESSING CHALLENGES AND MAINTAINING LONG-TERM SUCCESS:

i. Support and Education: Seek support from healthcare professionals, registered dietitians, or online communities specializing in low carb living. They can provide guidance, address your concerns, and help you navigate any challenges you may encounter along the way. Continuous education about low carb principles and staying up-to-

date with the latest research can also contribute to long-term success.

ii. Overcoming Plateaus: Weight loss plateaus and periods of slowed progress can happen on any dietary plan, including low carb diets. It's important to stay patient, evaluate your dietary choices, and consider adjustments such as modifying your macronutrient ratios, increasing physical activity, or seeking professional guidance to break through plateaus.

iii. Flexibility and Moderation: While low carb diets emphasize reducing carbohydrate intake, it's essential to find a balance that allows for flexibility and occasional indulgences. Allowing yourself the freedom to enjoy your favorite higher-carb foods in moderation can help you maintain long-term adherence to your low carb lifestyle.

Practical Application

A. MEAL PLANNING AND THE IMPORTANCE OF MINDFUL EATING:

i. Meal Planning: Meal planning is a key component of successful low carb living. By planning your meals in advance, you can ensure that you have nutritious, low carb options readily available, reducing the temptation to rely on high-carb convenience foods. Meal planning also allows you to balance your macronutrients and incorporate a variety of vegetables, proteins, and healthy fats into your diet.

ii. Portion Control: Mindful eating is crucial for portion control and preventing overeating. Take time to sit down and savor your meals, paying attention to hunger and fullness cues. Practice mindful eating by focusing on the flavors, textures, and enjoyment of each bite. This helps you cultivate a healthier relationship with food and prevents mindless snacking or emotional eating.

B. GROCERY SHOPPING TIPS FOR LOW CARB LIVING:

i. Stick to the Perimeter: When grocery shopping for low carb living, focus on shopping around the perimeter of the store. This is where you'll find fresh produce, lean meats, dairy products, and other whole foods. Minimize your time spent in the aisles that contain processed and high-carb foods.

ii. Read Food Labels: Become adept at reading food labels to identify hidden sources of carbohydrates. Look out for added sugars, refined grains, and high-carb ingredients in packaged foods. Aim for foods with minimal or no added sugars, and choose whole grains sparingly or opt for lower carb alternatives like almond flour or coconut flour.

C. MASTERING THE ART OF PREPARING DELICIOUS LOW CARB MEALS:

i. Experiment with Recipes: Explore a variety of low carb recipes to keep your meals interesting and enjoyable. Look for recipe resources like cookbooks, websites, and cooking blogs that focus on low carb or keto-friendly options. Experiment with different flavors, seasonings, and cooking techniques to add excitement to your low carb meals.

ii. Swap High-Carb Ingredients: Get creative and find low carb alternatives for your favorite high-carb ingredients.

For example, cauliflower can be riced or mashed as a substitute for grains, and zucchini noodles (zoodles) can replace traditional pasta. Discover the versatility of low carb ingredients like almond flour, coconut flour, and flaxseed meal in baking and cooking.

D. INCORPORATING MOVEMENT, STRESS MANAGEMENT, AND SELF-CARE INTO A HOLISTIC APPROACH:

i. Regular Exercise: Combine your low carb diet with regular physical activity to optimize overall health. Engage in activities you enjoy, such as walking, jogging, cycling, or strength training. Regular exercise not only supports weight management but also improves cardiovascular health, boosts mood, and enhances overall well-being.

ii. Stress Management: Stress can affect our eating habits and overall health. Incorporate stress management techniques such as meditation, deep breathing exercises, yoga, or engaging in hobbies and activities that help you relax and unwind. By managing stress, you can avoid stress-related eating and make mindful food choices.

iii. Self-Care: Prioritize self-care as an integral part of your low carb lifestyle. Get enough sleep, practice good sleep hygiene, and establish a regular sleep routine. Take time for activities that bring you joy and relaxation, such as reading, spending time in nature, or engaging in hobbies. Self-care helps reduce stress, promotes mental well-being, and supports overall health.

Adapting a Low Carb Diet for Specific Dietary Needs

VEGETARIAN AND VEGAN LOW-CARB DIETS

Plant-Based Protein Sources: Vegetarians can include protein-rich foods like eggs, dairy products, and plant-based protein sources such as legumes, tofu, tempeh, and edamame. Vegans can focus on plant-based protein options like legumes, tofu, tempeh, seitan, soy products, and textured vegetable protein (TVP).

Healthy Fats: Incorporate plant-based healthy fats such as avocados, nuts, seeds, and their respective oils. Plant-based oils like olive oil, coconut oil, and avocado oil can be used for cooking and dressings.

Nutrient-Rich Vegetables: Non-starchy vegetables like leafy greens, broccoli, cauliflower, zucchini, bell peppers, and mushrooms can form the foundation of meals, providing fiber, vitamins, and minerals.

Alternative Grains: Consider low-carb grain alternatives like quinoa, buckwheat, and amaranth, which are higher in protein and fiber compared to traditional grains.

Dairy Alternatives: For vegans or individuals with lactose intolerance, opt for plant-based milk alternatives like almond milk, coconut milk, or soy milk.

Recipe Adaptations: Modify low-carb recipes to remove animal products or replace them with suitable alternatives. Explore vegetarian or vegan cookbooks and online resources for inspiration.

GLUTEN-FREE LOW-CARB DIETS

Gluten-Free Grains: Choose naturally gluten-free low-carb grains such as quinoa, brown rice, buckwheat, millet, and amaranth.

Nut and Seed Flours: Replace wheat flour with almond flour, coconut flour, or flaxseed meal in baking to create gluten-free and low-carb recipes.

Vegetable Substitutions: Use vegetable alternatives for traditional gluten-containing foods, such as using zucchini noodles or cauliflower rice instead of pasta or rice.

Gluten-Free Protein Sources: Incorporate gluten-free protein sources like lean meats, poultry, fish, eggs, legumes, tofu, tempeh, and dairy products.

Check Labels: Be vigilant in reading food labels to identify hidden sources of gluten in packaged foods and condiments.

Gluten-Free Recipe Resources: Explore gluten-free recipe books, websites, and communities that focus on low-carb and gluten-free cooking.

FOOD ALLERGIES OR INTOLERANCES

Identify Trigger Foods: If you have food allergies or intolerances, be aware of ingredients that may cause adverse reactions and avoid them. Common allergens include dairy, eggs, nuts, shellfish, and soy.

Substitutions: Find suitable replacements for allergenic foods. For example, individuals with dairy allergies can opt for lactose-free or plant-based alternatives like almond milk or coconut yogurt.

Allergen-Free Recipes: Look for allergen-free recipes or modify existing low-carb recipes to exclude problematic ingredients. Many websites and cookbooks offer recipes specifically tailored to common allergens.

Nutrient Considerations: Ensure that nutrient needs are met by incorporating alternative food sources. Consult with a healthcare professional or registered dietitian to address specific nutritional concerns.

In conclusion, the low carb diet has gained significant attention for its potential benefits in weight management, blood sugar control, appetite control, and heart health. By limiting carbohydrate intake and focusing on nutrient-dense foods, individuals can experience positive changes in their overall health and well-being.

The principles of low carb living revolve around finding the right balance of carbohydrates, prioritizing protein and healthy fats, and embracing whole, unprocessed foods. Meal planning, mindful eating, and grocery shopping tips play a vital role in successfully adopting and maintaining a low carb lifestyle.

It is important to remember that individual needs and preferences may vary, and personalization is key to long-term success. Adapting low carb eating to fit your unique circumstances, incorporating ingredient variety and substitutions, and addressing challenges along the way will help create a sustainable and enjoyable approach to low carb living.

By focusing on finding balance, listening to your body, and making informed choices, you can harness the benefits of a low carb diet while promoting overall health and well-being. Remember, consulting with healthcare professionals or registered dietitians can provide personalized guidance and support on your low carb journey.

Embarking on a low carb lifestyle is not just a short-term fix, but a long-term commitment to your health. With dedication, flexibility, and a holistic approach encompassing movement, stress management, and self-care, you can embrace the benefits of low carb living and enjoy a healthier, happier life.

Chapter 3
28-day Meal Plan

Congratulations on taking the first step towards a healthier you! Embarking on a low carb diet can be challenging, but remember that you have the power to transform your eating habits and improve your well-being. Embrace this week as a fresh start, where you bid farewell to processed carbs and welcome wholesome alternatives. Focus on incorporating lean proteins, leafy greens, and healthy fats into your meals. It might be tough initially, but stay determined and remind yourself of the incredible benefits you will reap from this dietary shift. Your body will thank you, and the results will soon become evident.

Meal Plan	Breakfast	Snack	Lunch	Dinner	Snack
Day-1	Coconut Flour Bagels	Puffy Anise Cookies	Authentic Fennel Avgolemono	Saucy Mustard Salmon	Puffy Anise Cookies
	Kcal: 426 | Fat: 19.1g | Net Carbs: 0.4g | Protein: 33.1g	Calories: 142 | Fat: 13g | Carbs: 5.2g | Protein: 3.5g | Fiber: 2.4g	Calories: 86 | Fat: 6.1g | Carbs: 6g | Protein: 2.8g | Fiber: 2.4g	Cal: 537 | Fat: 26.4g | Net Carbs: 1.5g | Protein 67g	Calories: 142 | Fat: 13g | Carbs: 5.2g | Protein: 3.5g | Fiber: 2.4g
Day-2	Coconut Flour Bagels	Puffy Anise Cookies	Authentic Fennel Avgolemono	Saucy Mustard Salmon	Puffy Anise Cookies
	Kcal: 426 | Fat: 19.1g | Net Carbs: 0.4g | Protein: 33.1g	Calories: 142 | Fat: 13g | Carbs: 5.2g | Protein: 3.5g | Fiber: 2.4g	Calories: 86 | Fat: 6.1g | Carbs: 6g | Protein: 2.8g | Fiber: 2.4g	Cal: 537 | Fat: 26.4g | Net Carbs: 1.5g | Protein 67g	Calories: 142 | Fat: 13g | Carbs: 5.2g | Protein: 3.5g | Fiber: 2.4g
Day-3	Coconut Flour Bagels	Puffy Anise Cookies	Authentic Fennel Avgolemono	Saucy Mustard Salmon	Puffy Anise Cookies
	Kcal: 426 | Fat: 19.1g | Net Carbs: 0.4g | Protein: 33.1g	Calories: 142 | Fat: 13g | Carbs: 5.2g | Protein: 3.5g | Fiber: 2.4g	Calories: 86 | Fat: 6.1g | Carbs: 6g | Protein: 2.8g | Fiber: 2.4g	Cal: 537 | Fat: 26.4g | Net Carbs: 1.5g | Protein 67g	Calories: 142 | Fat: 13g | Carbs: 5.2g | Protein: 3.5g | Fiber: 2.4g
Day-4	Coconut Flour Bagels	Puffy Anise Cookies	Authentic Fennel Avgolemono	Saucy Mustard Salmon	Puffy Anise Cookies
	Kcal: 426 | Fat: 19.1g | Net Carbs: 0.4g | Protein: 33.1g	Calories: 142 | Fat: 13g | Carbs: 5.2g | Protein: 3.5g | Fiber: 2.4g	Calories: 86 | Fat: 6.1g | Carbs: 6g | Protein: 2.8g | Fiber: 2.4g	Cal: 537 | Fat: 26.4g | Net Carbs: 1.5g | Protein 67g	Calories: 142 | Fat: 13g | Carbs: 5.2g | Protein: 3.5g | Fiber: 2.4g
Day-5	Cheesy Turkey Sausage Egg Muffins	Puffy Anise Cookies	Authentic Fennel Avgolemono	Fluffy Chicken	Puffy Anise Cookies

	Breakfast	Snack	Lunch	Dinner	Snack
	Kcal: 423 | Fat: 34.1g | Net Carbs: 2.2g | Protein: 26.5g	Calories: 142 | Fat: 13g | Carbs: 5.2g | Protein: 3.5g | Fiber: 2.4g	Calories: 86 | Fat: 6.1g | Carbs: 6g | Protein: 2.8g | Fiber: 2.4g	Calories: 325 | Fat: 16g | Protein: 33g | Fiber: 0g |Carbs: 3g	Calories: 142 | Fat: 13g | Carbs: 5.2g | Protein: 3.5g | Fiber: 2.4g
Day-6	Cheesy Turkey Sausage Egg Muffins	Hot Chard Artichoke Dip	Authentic Fennel Avgolemono	Fluffy Chicken	Hot Chard Artichoke Dip
	Kcal: 423 | Fat: 34.1g | Net Carbs: 2.2g | Protein: 26.5g	Calories: 280 | Total Fat: 25g | Total Carbs: 5g | Fiber: 1g | Protein: 11g	Calories: 86 | Fat: 6.1g | Carbs: 6g | Protein: 2.8g | Fiber: 2.4g	Calories: 325 | Fat: 16g | Protein: 33g | Fiber: 0g |Carbs: 3g	Calories: 280 | Total Fat: 25g | Total Carbs: 5g | Fiber: 1g | Protein: 11g
Day-7	Cheesy Turkey Sausage Egg Muffins	Hot Chard Artichoke Dip	Fluffy Chicken	Fluffy Chicken	Hot Chard Artichoke Dip
	Kcal: 423 | Fat: 34.1g | Net Carbs: 2.2g | Protein: 26.5g	Calories: 280 | Total Fat: 25g | Total Carbs: 5g | Fiber: 1g | Protein: 11g	Calories: 325 | Fat: 16g | Protein: 33g | Fiber: 0g |Carbs: 3g	Calories: 325 | Fat: 16g | Protein: 33g | Fiber: 0g |Carbs: 3g	Calories: 280 | Total Fat: 25g | Total Carbs: 5g | Fiber: 1g | Protein: 11g

Week 2

You've made it through the first week, and now it's time to build momentum. As you continue on your low carb journey, you'll likely notice some positive changes: increased energy, improved mental clarity, and even some weight loss. This week, let's take it up a notch. Experiment with new recipes that excite your taste buds while still adhering to the low carb principles. Seek inspiration from colorful vegetables, nourishing seafood, and vibrant spices. Remember, your commitment to this healthier lifestyle is forging a path towards long-term well-being. Stay focused, and keep pushing forward!

Meal Plan	Breakfast	Snack	Lunch	Dinner	Snack
Day-1	Cheesy Sausage Quiche	Chocolate Almond Squares	Peasant Stir-Fry (Satarash)	Drunken Pot Roast	Chocolate Almond Squares
	Kcal: 340 | Fat: 28g | Net Carbs: 3g | Protein: 17g	Calories: 234 | Fat: 25.1g | Carbs: 3.6g | Protein: 1.7g | Fiber: 1.4g	Calories: 114 | Fat: 7.6g | Carbs: 6g | Protein: 3.4g | Fiber: 1.5g	Calories: 556 | Fat: 34g | Protein: 49g | Fiber: 0g | Net Carbs: 4g	Calories: 234 | Fat: 25.1g | Carbs: 3.6g | Protein: 1.7g | Fiber: 1.4g
Day-2	Cheesy Sausage Quiche	Chocolate Almond Squares	Peasant Stir-Fry (Satarash)	Drunken Pot Roast	Chocolate Almond Squares

	Kcal: 340 | Fat: 28g | Net Carbs: 3g | Protein: 17g	Calories: 234 | Fat: 25.1g | Carbs: 3.6g | Protein: 1.7g | Fiber: 1.4g	Calories: 114 | Fat: 7.6g | Carbs: 6g | Protein: 3.4g | Fiber: 1.5g	Calories: 556 | Fat: 34g | Protein: 49g | Fiber: 0g | Net Carbs: 4g	Calories: 234 | Fat: 25.1g | Carbs: 3.6g | Protein: 1.7g | Fiber: 1.4g
Day-3	Cheesy Sausage Quiche	Chocolate Almond Squares	Peasant Stir-Fry (Satarash)	Drunken Pot Roast	Chocolate Almond Squares
	Kcal: 340 | Fat: 28g | Net Carbs: 3g | Protein: 17g	Calories: 234 | Fat: 25.1g | Carbs: 3.6g | Protein: 1.7g | Fiber: 1.4g	Calories: 114 | Fat: 7.6g | Carbs: 6g | Protein: 3.4g | Fiber: 1.5g	Calories: 556 | Fat: 34g | Protein: 49g | Fiber: 0g | Net Carbs: 4g	Calories: 234 | Fat: 25.1g | Carbs: 3.6g | Protein: 1.7g | Fiber: 1.4g
Day-4	Cheesy Sausage Quiche	Chocolate Almond Squares	Peasant Stir-Fry (Satarash)	Drunken Pot Roast	Chocolate Almond Squares
	Kcal: 340 | Fat: 28g | Net Carbs: 3g | Protein: 17g	Calories: 234 | Fat: 25.1g | Carbs: 3.6g | Protein: 1.7g | Fiber: 1.4g	Calories: 114 | Fat: 7.6g | Carbs: 6g | Protein: 3.4g | Fiber: 1.5g	Calories: 556 | Fat: 34g | Protein: 49g | Fiber: 0g | Net Carbs: 4g	Calories: 234 | Fat: 25.1g | Carbs: 3.6g | Protein: 1.7g | Fiber: 1.4g
Day-5	Cheesy Sausage Quiche	Chocolate Almond Squares	Peasant Stir-Fry (Satarash)	Drunken Pot Roast	Chocolate Almond Squares
	Kcal: 340 | Fat: 28g | Net Carbs: 3g | Protein: 17g	Calories: 234 | Fat: 25.1g | Carbs: 3.6g | Protein: 1.7g | Fiber: 1.4g	Calories: 114 | Fat: 7.6g | Carbs: 6g | Protein: 3.4g | Fiber: 1.5g	Calories: 556 | Fat: 34g | Protein: 49g | Fiber: 0g | Net Carbs: 4g	Calories: 234 | Fat: 25.1g | Carbs: 3.6g | Protein: 1.7g | Fiber: 1.4g
Day-6	Cheesy Sausage Quiche	Warm Herbed Olives	Drunken Pot Roast	Drunken Pot Roast	Warm Herbed Olives
	Kcal: 340 | Fat: 28g | Net Carbs: 3g | Protein: 17g	Calories: 165 | Total Fat: 17g | Total Carbs: 3g | Fiber: 1g | Protein: 1g	Calories: 556 | Fat: 34g | Protein: 49g | Fiber: 0g | Net Carbs: 4g	Calories: 556 | Fat: 34g | Protein: 49g | Fiber: 0g | Net Carbs: 4g	Calories: 165 | Total Fat: 17g | Total Carbs: 3g | Fiber: 1g | Protein: 1g
Day-7	Hashed Zucchini & Bacon Breakfast	Warm Herbed Olives	Jerked Beef Stew	Jerked Beef Stew	Warm Herbed Olives
	Kcal: 340 | Fat: 26.8g | Net Carbs: 6.6g | Protein: 17.4g	Calories: 165 | Total Fat: 17g | Total Carbs: 3g | Fiber: 1g | Protein: 1g	Cal: 235 | Fat: 13.4g | Net Carbs: 2.8g | Protein 25.8g	Cal: 235 | Fat: 13.4g | Net Carbs: 2.8g | Protein 25.8g	Calories: 165 | Total Fat: 17g | Total Carbs: 3g | Fiber: 1g | Protein: 1g

You're doing amazing! By now, you've experienced the transformative power of a low carb diet, and it's time to take things to the next level. This week, let's fine-tune your meal plan and optimize your nutrient intake. Consider incorporating more plant-based proteins like tofu or lentils, along with a variety of nuts and seeds for added crunch and healthy fats. Explore the world of low carb snacks and find options that satisfy your cravings without derailing your progress. Trust the process, stay disciplined, and remind yourself that each day brings you closer to your health goals.

Meal Plan	Breakfast	Snack	Lunch	Dinner	Snack
Day-1	Cauliflower & Cheese Burgers	No Bake Energy Bites	Superb Mushroom Mélange	Flank Steak Roll	No Bake Energy Bites
	Kcal: 416 | Fat: 33.8g | Net Carbs: 7.8g | Protein: 13g	Calories: 102 | Fat: 7.8g | Carbs: 5.8g | Protein: 2.6g | Fiber: 1.8g	Calories: 123 | Fat: 9.2g | Carbs: 5.8g | Protein: 4.7g | Fiber: 1.4g	Cal: 445 | Fat: 21g | Net Carbs: 2.8g | Protein 53g	Calories: 102 | Fat: 7.8g | Carbs: 5.8g | Protein: 2.6g | Fiber: 1.8g
Day-2	Cauliflower & Cheese Burgers	No Bake Energy Bites	Superb Mushroom Mélange	Flank Steak Roll	No Bake Energy Bites
	Kcal: 416 | Fat: 33.8g | Net Carbs: 7.8g | Protein: 13g	Calories: 102 | Fat: 7.8g | Carbs: 5.8g | Protein: 2.6g | Fiber: 1.8g	Calories: 123 | Fat: 9.2g | Carbs: 5.8g | Protein: 4.7g | Fiber: 1.4g	Cal: 445 | Fat: 21g | Net Carbs: 2.8g | Protein 53g	Calories: 102 | Fat: 7.8g | Carbs: 5.8g | Protein: 2.6g | Fiber: 1.8g
Day-3	Cauliflower & Cheese Burgers	No Bake Energy Bites	Superb Mushroom Mélange	Flank Steak Roll	No Bake Energy Bites
	Kcal: 416 | Fat: 33.8g | Net Carbs: 7.8g | Protein: 13g	Calories: 102 | Fat: 7.8g | Carbs: 5.8g | Protein: 2.6g | Fiber: 1.8g	Calories: 123 | Fat: 9.2g | Carbs: 5.8g | Protein: 4.7g | Fiber: 1.4g	Cal: 445 | Fat: 21g | Net Carbs: 2.8g | Protein 53g	Calories: 102 | Fat: 7.8g | Carbs: 5.8g | Protein: 2.6g | Fiber: 1.8g
Day-4	Cauliflower & Cheese Burgers	No Bake Energy Bites	Superb Mushroom Mélange	Flank Steak Roll	No Bake Energy Bites
	Kcal: 416 | Fat: 33.8g | Net Carbs: 7.8g | Protein: 13g	Calories: 102 | Fat: 7.8g | Carbs: 5.8g | Protein: 2.6g | Fiber: 1.8g	Calories: 123 | Fat: 9.2g | Carbs: 5.8g | Protein: 4.7g | Fiber: 1.4g	Cal: 445 | Fat: 21g | Net Carbs: 2.8g | Protein 53g	Calories: 102 | Fat: 7.8g | Carbs: 5.8g | Protein: 2.6g | Fiber: 1.8g
Day-5	Cauliflower & Cheese Burgers	No Bake Energy Bites	Superb Mushroom Mélange	Mustardy Crab Cakes	No Bake Energy Bites
	Kcal: 416 | Fat: 33.8g | Net Carbs: 7.8g | Protein: 13g	Calories: 102 | Fat: 7.8g | Carbs: 5.8g | Protein: 2.6g | Fiber: 1.8g	Calories: 123 | Fat: 9.2g | Carbs: 5.8g | Protein: 4.7g | Fiber: 1.4g	Cal: 315 | Fat: 24.5g | Net Carbs: 1.6g | Protein 15.3g	Calories: 102 | Fat: 7.8g | Carbs: 5.8g | Protein: 2.6g | Fiber: 1.8g

Day-6	Cauliflower & Cheese Burgers	Cheesecake Fat Bombs	Superb Mushroom Mélange	Mustardy Crab Cakes	Cheesecake Fat Bombs
	Kcal: 416 | Fat: 33.8g | Net Carbs: 7.8g | Protein: 13g	Calories: 406 | Fat: 40.5g | Carbs: 6.7g | Protein: 7.5g | Fiber: 2.5g	Calories: 123 | Fat: 9.2g | Carbs: 5.8g | Protein: 4.7g | Fiber: 1.4g	Cal: 315 | Fat: 24.5g | Net Carbs: 1.6g | Protein 15.3g	Calories: 406 | Fat: 40.5g | Carbs: 6.7g | Protein: 7.5g | Fiber: 2.5g
Day-7	Morning Almond Shake	Cheesecake Fat Bombs	Mustardy Crab Cakes	Mustardy Crab Cakes	Cheesecake Fat Bombs
	Kcal: 326 | Fat: 27g | Net Carbs: 6g | Protein: 19g	Calories: 406 | Fat: 40.5g | Carbs: 6.7g | Protein: 7.5g | Fiber: 2.5g	Cal: 315 | Fat: 24.5g | Net Carbs: 1.6g | Protein 15.3g	Cal: 315 | Fat: 24.5g | Net Carbs: 1.6g | Protein 15.3g	Calories: 406 | Fat: 40.5g | Carbs: 6.7g | Protein: 7.5g | Fiber: 2.5g

Week 4

You've reached the final week of your low carb meal plan, and your dedication has paid off. Take a moment to reflect on how far you've come. Notice the increased vitality, improved digestion, and perhaps even a few inches shed from your waistline. As you approach the finish line, it's important to maintain your focus and continue making mindful choices. Plan your meals with intention, choosing whole foods that nourish your body and support your long-term well-being. Remember, this is not just a temporary diet but a lifestyle change. Embrace the empowerment that comes with knowing you have the ability to create lasting positive change in your life. You've got this!

Meal Plan	Breakfast	Snack	Lunch	Dinner	Snack
Day-1	Bacon Tomato Cups	Peanut Butter and Chocolate Treat	Summer Mediterranean Salad	Chimichurri Tiger Shrimp	Peanut Butter and Chocolate Treat
	Kcal: 425 | Fat: 45.2g | Net Carbs: 4.3g | Protein: 16.2g	Calories: 122 | Fat: 11.7g | Carbs: 4.9g | Fiber: 1.4g | Protein: 1.5g	Calories: 243 | Fat: 22.2g | Carbs: 6.8g | Protein: 6.5g | Fiber: 1.9g	Cal: 523 | Fat: 30.3g | Net Carbs: 7.2g | Protein 49g	Calories: 122 | Fat: 11.7g | Carbs: 4.9g | Fiber: 1.4g | Protein: 1.5g
Day-2	Bacon Tomato Cups	Peanut Butter and Chocolate Treat	Summer Mediterranean Salad	Chimichurri Tiger Shrimp	Peanut Butter and Chocolate Treat
	Kcal: 425 | Fat: 45.2g | Net Carbs: 4.3g | Protein: 16.2g	Calories: 122 | Fat: 11.7g | Carbs: 4.9g | Protein: 1.5g	Calories: 243 | Fat: 22.2g | Carbs: 6.8g | Protein: 6.5g | Fiber: 1.9g	Cal: 523 | Fat: 30.3g | Net Carbs: 7.2g | Protein 49g	Calories: 122 | Fat: 11.7g | Carbs: 4.9g | Fiber: 1.4g | Protein: 1.5g

Day-3	Bacon Tomato Cups	Peanut Butter and Chocolate Treat	Summer Mediterranean Salad	Chimichurri Tiger Shrimp	Peanut Butter and Chocolate Treat
	Kcal: 425 | Fat: 45.2g | Net Carbs: 4.3g | Protein: 16.2g	Calories: 122 | Fat: 11.7g | Carbs: 4.9g | Fiber: 1.4g | Protein: 1.5g	Calories: 243 | Fat: 22.2g | Carbs: 6.8g | Protein: 6.5g | Fiber: 1.9g	Cal: 523 | Fat: 30.3g | Net Carbs: 7.2g | Protein 49g	Calories: 122 | Fat: 11.7g | Carbs: 4.9g | Fiber: 1.4g | Protein: 1.5g
Day-4	Bacon Tomato Cups	Peanut Butter and Chocolate Treat	Summer Mediterranean Salad	Chimichurri Tiger Shrimp	Peanut Butter and Chocolate Treat
	Kcal: 425 | Fat: 45.2g | Net Carbs: 4.3g | Protein: 16.2g	Calories: 122 | Fat: 11.7g | Carbs: 4.9g | Fiber: 1.4g | Protein: 1.5g	Calories: 243 | Fat: 22.2g | Carbs: 6.8g | Protein: 6.5g | Fiber: 1.9g	Cal: 523 | Fat: 30.3g | Net Carbs: 7.2g | Protein 49g	Calories: 122 | Fat: 11.7g | Carbs: 4.9g | Fiber: 1.4g | Protein: 1.5g
Day-5	Bacon Tomato Cups	Peanut Butter and Chocolate Treat	Creole Beef Tripe Stew	Creole Beef Tripe Stew	Peanut Butter and Chocolate Treat
	Kcal: 425 | Fat: 45.2g | Net Carbs: 4.3g | Protein: 16.2g	Calories: 122 | Fat: 11.7g | Carbs: 4.9g | Fiber: 1.4g | Protein: 1.5g	Cal: 342 | Net Carbs: 1g | Fat: 27g | Protein 22g	Cal: 342 | Net Carbs: 1g | Fat: 27g | Protein 22g	Calories: 122 | Fat: 11.7g | Carbs: 4.9g | Fiber: 1.4g | Protein: 1.5g
Day-6	Breakfast Buttered Eggs	Strawberry Cream Ice Pops	Creole Beef Tripe Stew	Creole Beef Tripe Stew	Strawberry Cream Ice Pops
	Kcal: 321 | Fat: 21.5g | Net Carbs: 2.5g | Protein: 12.8g	Calories: 175 | Fat: 16.5 g | Protein: 1 g | Total Carbs: 8 g | Net Carbs: 3.8 g	Cal: 342 | Net Carbs: 1g | Fat: 27g | Protein 22g	Cal: 342 | Net Carbs: 1g | Fat: 27g | Protein 22g	Calories: 175 | Fat: 16.5 g | Protein: 1 g | Total Carbs: 8 g | Net Carbs: 3.8 g
Day-7	Breakfast Buttered Eggs	Strawberry Cream Ice Pops	Creole Beef Tripe Stew	Creole Beef Tripe Stew	Strawberry Cream Ice Pops
	Kcal: 321 | Fat: 21.5g | Net Carbs: 2.5g | Protein: 12.8g	Calories: 175 | Fat: 16.5 g | Protein: 1 g | Total Carbs: 8 g | Net Carbs: 3.8 g	Cal: 342 | Net Carbs: 1g | Fat: 27g | Protein 22g	Cal: 342 | Net Carbs: 1g | Fat: 27g | Protein 22g	Calories: 175 | Fat: 16.5 g | Protein: 1 g | Total Carbs: 8 g | Net Carbs: 3.8 g

Chapter 4
Breakfast

Breakfast Nut Granola & Smoothie Bowl

Prep time: 5 minutes | Cook time: 5 minutes | Serves 4

- 6 cups Greek yogurt
- 4 tbsp almond butter
- A handful toasted walnuts
- 3 tbsp unsweetened cocoa powder
- 4 tsp swerve brown sugar
- 2 cups nut granola for topping

1. Combine the Greek yogurt, almond butter, walnuts, cocoa powder, and swerve brown sugar in a smoothie maker; puree in high-speed until smooth and well mixed.
2. Share the smoothie into four breakfast bowls, top with a half cup of granola each, and serve.

PER SERVING

Kcal: 361 | Fat: 31.2g | Net Carbs: 2g | Protein: 13g

Bacon and Egg Quesadillas

Prep time: 30 minutes | Cook time: 6 minutes | Serves 4

- 8 low carb tortilla shells
- 6 eggs
- 1 cup water
- 3 tbsp butter
- 1 ½ cups grated cheddar cheese
- 1 ½ cups grated Swiss cheese
- 5 bacon slices
- 1 medium onion, thinly sliced
- 1 tbsp chopped parsley

1. Bring the eggs to a boil in water over medium heat for 10 minutes. Transfer the eggs to an ice water bath, peel the shells, and chop them; set aside.
2. Meanwhile, as the eggs cook, fry the bacon in a skillet over medium heat for 4 minutes until crispy. Remove and chop. Plate and set aside too.
3. Fetch out 2/3 of the bacon fat and sauté the onions in the remaining grease over medium heat for 2 minutes; set aside. Melt 1 tablespoon of butter in a skillet over medium heat.
4. Lay one tortilla in a skillet; sprinkle with some Swiss cheese. Add some chopped eggs and bacon over the cheese, top with onion, and sprinkle with some cheddar cheese. Cover with another tortilla shell. Cook for 45 seconds, then carefully flip the quesadilla, and cook the other side too for 45 seconds. Remove to a plate and repeat the cooking process using the remaining tortilla shells.
5. Garnish with parsley and serve warm.

PER SERVING

Kcal: 449 | Fat: 48.7g | Net Carbs: 6.8g | Protein: 29.1g

Avocado and Kale Eggs

Prep time: 20 minutes | Cook time: 11 minutes | Serves 4

- 1 tsp ghee
- 1 red onion, sliced
- 4 oz chorizo, sliced into thin rounds
- 1 cup chopped kale
- 1 ripe avocado, pitted, peeled, chopped
- 4 eggs
- Salt and black pepper to season

1. Preheat oven to 370°F.
2. Melt ghee in a cast iron pan over medium heat and sauté the onion for 2 minutes. Add the chorizo and cook for 2 minutes more, flipping once.
3. Introduce the kale in batches with a splash of water to wilt, season lightly with salt, stir and cook for 3 minutes. Mix in the avocado and turn the heat off.
4. Create four holes in the mixture, crack the eggs into each hole, sprinkle with salt and black pepper, and slide the pan into the preheated oven to bake for 6 minutes until the egg whites are set or firm and yolks still runny. Season to taste with salt and pepper, and serve right away with low carb toasts.

PER SERVING

Kcal: 274 | Fat: 23g | Net Carbs: 4g | Protein: 13g

Bacon and Cheese Frittata

Prep time: 25 minutes | Cook time: 16 minutes | Serves 4

- 10 slices bacon
- 10 fresh eggs
- 3 tbsp butter, melted
- ½ cup almond milk
- Salt and black pepper to taste
- 1 ½ cups cheddar cheese, shredded
- ¼ cup chopped green onions

1. Preheat the oven to 400°F and grease a baking dish with cooking spray. Cook the bacon in a skillet over medium heat for 6 minutes. Once crispy, remove from the skillet to paper towels and discard grease. Chop into small pieces. Whisk the eggs, butter, milk, salt, and black pepper. Mix in the bacon and pour the mixture into the baking dish.
2. Sprinkle with cheddar cheese and green onions, and bake in the oven for 10 minutes or until the eggs are thoroughly cooked. Remove and cool the frittata for 3 minutes, slice into wedges, and serve warm with a dollop of Greek yogurt.

PER SERVING

Kcal: 325 | Fat: 28g | Net Carbs: 2g | Protein: 15g

Egg in a Cheesy Spinach Nests

Prep time: 35 minutes | Cook time: 17 minutes | Serves 4

- 2 tbsp olive oil
- 1 clove garlic, grated
- ½ lb spinach, chopped
- Salt and black pepper to taste
- 2 tbsp shredded Parmesan cheese
- 2 tbsp shredded gouda cheese
- 4 eggs

1. Preheat oven to 350°F. Warm the oil in a non-stick skillet over medium heat; add the garlic and sauté until softened for 2 minutes. Add the spinach to wilt for about 5 minutes, and season with salt and black pepper. Allow cooling.
2. Grease a baking sheet with cooking spray, mold 4 (firm and separate) spinach nests on the sheet, and crack an egg into each nest. Sprinkle with Parmesan and gouda cheese. Bake for 15 minutes just until the egg whites have set and the yolks are still runny. Plate the nests and serve right away with low carb toasts and coffee.

PER SERVING

Kcal: 230 | Fat: 17.5g | Net Carbs: 4g | Protein: 12g

Coconut Flour Bagels

Prep time: 25 minutes | Cook time: 20 minutes | Serves 4

- ½ cup coconut flour
- 6 eggs, beaten in a bowl
- ½ cup vegetable broth
- ¼ cup flax seed meal
- ¼ cup chia seed meal
- 1 tsp onion powder
- 1 tsp garlic powder
- 1 tsp dried parsley
- 1 tsp chia seeds
- 1 tsp sesame seeds 1 chopped onion

1. Preheat the oven to 350°F.
2. Mix the coconut flour, eggs, broth, flax seed meal, chia seed meal, onion powder, garlic powder, and parsley. Spoon the mixture into a donut tray.
3. In a small bowl, mix the chia seeds, sesame seeds, and onion, and sprinkle on the batter.
4. Bake the bagels for 20 minutes. Serve the bagels with creamy pumpkin soup.

PER SERVING

Kcal: 426 | Fat: 19.1g | Net Carbs: 0.4g | Protein: 33.1g

Breakfast Bake

Prep time: 10 minutes | Cook time: 50 minutes | Serves 8

- 1 tablespoon olive oil, plus extra for greasing the casserole dish
- 1 pound preservative-free or homemade sausage
- 8 large eggs
- 2 cups cooked spaghetti squash
- 1 tablespoon chopped fresh oregano
- Sea salt
- Freshly ground black pepper
- ½ cup shredded Cheddar cheese

1. Preheat the oven to 375°F. Lightly grease a 9-by-13-inch casserole dish with olive oil and set aside.
2. Place a large ovenproof skillet over medium-high heat and add the olive oil.
3. Brown the sausage until cooked through, about 5 minutes. While the sausage is cooking, whisk together the eggs, squash, and oregano in a medium bowl. Season lightly with salt and pepper and set aside.
4. Add the cooked sausage to the egg mixture, stir until just combined, and pour the mixture into the casserole dish.
5. Sprinkle the top of the casserole with the cheese and cover the casserole loosely with aluminum foil.
6. Bake the casserole for 30 minutes, and then remove the foil and bake for an additional 15 minutes.
7. Let the casserole stand for 10 minutes before serving.

PER SERVING

Calories: 303 | Fat: 24g | Protein: 17g | Carbs: 4g | Fiber: 1g | Net Carbs: 3g

Spicy Egg Muffins with Bacon & Cheese

Prep time: 30 minutes | Cook time: 18 to 20 minutes | Serves 6

- 12 eggs
- ¼ cup coconut milk
- Salt and black pepper to taste
- 1 cup grated cheddar cheese
- 12 slices bacon
- 4 jalapeño peppers, seeded and minced

1. Preheat oven to 370°F.
2. Crack the eggs into a bowl and whisk with coconut milk until combined. Season with salt and pepper, and evenly stir in the cheddar cheese.
3. Line each hole of a muffin tin with a slice of bacon and fill each with the egg mixture twothirds way up. Top with the jalapeno peppers and bake in the oven for 18 to 20 minutes or until puffed and golden. Remove, allow cooling for a few minutes, and serve with arugula salad.

PER SERVING

Kcal: 302 | Fat: 23.7g | Net Carbs: 3.2g | Protein: 20g

Bacon Tomato Cups

Prep time: 33 minutes | Cook time: 18 minutes | Serves 6

- 12 bacon slices
- 2 tomatoes, diced
- 1 onion, diced
- 1 cup shredded cheddar cheese
- 1 cup mayonnaise
- 12 low carb crepes/pancakes
- 1 tsp dried basil
- Chopped chives to garnish

1. Fry the bacon in a skillet over medium heat for 5 minutes. Remove and chop with a knife. Transfer to a bowl. Add in cheddar cheese, tomatoes, onion, mayonnaise, and basil. Mix well set aside.
2. Place the crepes on a flat surface and use egg rings to cut a circle out of each crepe. Grease the muffin cups with cooking spray and fit the circled crepes into them to make a cup.
3. Now, fill the cups with 3 tbsp of bacon-tomato mixture. Place the muffin cups on a baking sheet, and bake for 18 minutes. Garnish with the chives, and serve with a tomato or cheese sauce.

PER SERVING

Kcal: 425 | Fat: 45.2g | Net Carbs: 4.3g | Protein: 16.2g

Cheesy Sausage Quiche

Prep time: 55 minutes | Cook time: 40 minutes | Serves 6

- 6 eggs
- 12 ounces raw sausage roll
- 10 cherry tomatoes, halved
- 2 tbsp heavy cream
- 2 tbsp Parmesan cheese
- ¼ tsp salt
- A pinch of black pepper
- 2 tbsp chopped parsley
- 5 eggplant slices

1. Preheat your oven to 370°F.
2. Grease a pie dish with cooking spray. Press the sausage roll at the bottom of a pie dish. Arrange the eggplant slices on top of the sausage. Top with cherry tomatoes.
3. Whisk the eggs along with the heavy cream, salt, Parmesan cheese, and black pepper. Spoon the mixture over the sausage. Bake for about 40 minutes until browned around the edges. Serve warm, sprinkled with parsley.

PER SERVING

Kcal: 340 | Fat: 28g | Net Carbs: 3g | Protein: 17g

Creamy Cinnamon Smoothie

Prep time: 5 minutes | Cook time: 15 minutes | Serves 2

- 2 cups coconut milk
- 1 scoop vanilla protein powder
- 5 drops liquid stevia
- 1 teaspoon ground cinnamon
- ½ teaspoon alcohol-free vanilla extract

1. Put the coconut milk, protein powder, stevia, cinnamon, and vanilla in a blender and blend until smooth.
2. Pour into 2 glasses and serve immediately.

PER SERVING

Calories: 492 | Fat: 47g | Protein: 18g | Carbs: 8g | Fiber: 2g | Net Carbs: 6g

Cheesy Turkey Sausage Egg Muffins

Prep time: 15 minutes | Cook time: 5 minutes | Serves 3

- 1 tsp butter
- 6 eggs
- Salt and black pepper, to taste
- ½ tsp dried rosemary
- 1 cup pecorino romano cheese, grated
- 3 turkey sausages, chopped

1. Preheat oven to 400°F and grease muffin cups with cooking spray.
2. In a skillet over medium heat add the butter and cook the turkey sausages for 4-5 minutes.
3. Beat 3 eggs with a fork. Add in sausages, cheese, and seasonings. Divide between the muffin cups and bake for 4 minutes. Crack in an egg to each of the cups. Bake for an additional 4 minutes. Allow cooling before serving.

PER SERVING

Kcal: 423 | Fat: 34.1g | Net Carbs: 2.2g | Protein: 26.5g

Spinach-Blueberry Smoothie

Prep time: 5 minutes | Cook time: 15 minutes | Serves 2

- 1 cup coconut milk
- 1 cup spinach
- ½ English cucumber, chopped
- ½ cup blueberries
- 1 scoop plain protein powder
- 2 tablespoons coconut oil
- 4 ice cubes
- Mint sprigs, for garnish

1. Put the coconut milk, spinach, cucumber, blueberries, protein powder, coconut oil, and ice in a blender and blend until smooth.
2. Pour into 2 glasses, garnish each with the mint, and serve immediately.

PER SERVING

Calories: 353 | Fat: 32g | Protein: 15g | Carbs: 9g | Fiber: 3g | Net Carbs: 6g

Almond Waffles with Cinnamon Cream

Prep time: 25 minutes | Cook time: 15 minutes | Serves 6

FOR THE SPREAD
- 8 oz cream cheese, at room temperature
- 1 tsp cinnamon powder
- 3 tbsp swerve brown sugar
- Cinnamon powder for garnishing
- For The Waffles
- 5 tbsp melted butter
- 1½ cups unsweetened almond milk
- 7 large eggs
- ¼ tsp liquid stevia
- ½ tsp baking powder
- 1½ cups almond flour

1. Combine the cream cheese, cinnamon, and swerve with a hand mixer until smooth. Cover and chill until ready to use.
2. To make the waffles, whisk the butter, milk, and eggs in a medium bowl. Add the stevia and baking powder and mix. Stir in the almond flour and combine until no lumps exist. Let the batter sit for 5 minutes to thicken. Spritz a waffle iron with a non-stick cooking spray. Ladle a ¼ cup of the batter into the waffle iron and cook according to the manufacturer's instructions until golden, about 10 minutes in total. Repeat with the remaining batter.
3. Slice the waffles into quarters; apply the cinnamon spread in between each of two waffles and snap. Sprinkle with cinnamon powder and serve.

PER SERVING

Kcal: 307 | Fat: 24g | Net Carbs: 8g | Protein: 12g

Mushroom Frittata

Prep time: 10 minutes | Cook time: 15 minutes | Serves 6

- 2 tablespoons olive oil
- 1 cup sliced fresh mushrooms
- 1 cup shredded spinach
- 6 bacon slices, cooked and chopped
- 10 large eggs, beaten
- ½ cup crumbled goat cheese
- Sea salt
- Freshly ground black pepper

1. Preheat the oven to 350°F.
2. Place a large ovenproof skillet over medium-high heat and add the olive oil.
3. Sauté the mushrooms until lightly browned, about 3 minutes.
4. Add the spinach and bacon and sauté until the greens are wilted, about 1 minute.
5. Add the eggs and cook, lifting the edges of the frittata with a spatula so uncooked egg flows underneath, for 3 to 4 minutes.
6. Sprinkle the top with the crumbled goat cheese and season lightly with salt and pepper.
7. Bake until set and lightly browned, about 15 minutes.
8. Remove the frittata from the oven, and let it stand for 5 minutes.
9. Cut into 6 wedges and serve immediately.

PER SERVING

Calories: 316 | Fat: 27g | Protein: 16g | Carbs: 1g | Fiber: 0g | Net Carbs: 1g

Breakfast Buttered Eggs

Prep time: 15 minutes | Cook time: 7 minutes | Serves 2

- 1 tbsp coconut oil
- 2 tbsp butter
- 1 tsp fresh thyme
- 4 eggs
- 2 garlic cloves, minced
- ½ cup chopped parsley
- ½ cup chopped cilantro
- ¼ tsp cumin
- ¼ tsp cayenne pepper
- Salt and black pepper, to taste

1. Drizzle the coconut oil into a non-stick skillet over medium heat. Once the oil is warm, add the butter, and melt. Add garlic and thyme and cook for 30 seconds. Sprinkle with parsley and cilantro; and cook for another 2 minutes, until crisp.
2. Carefully crack the eggs into the skillet. Lower the heat and cook for 4-6 minutes. Season with salt, black pepper, cumin, and cayenne pepper. When the eggs are just set, turn the heat off and transfer to a serving plate.

PER SERVING

Kcal: 321 | Fat: 21.5g | Net Carbs: 2.5g | Protein: 12.8g

Hashed Zucchini & Bacon Breakfast

Prep time: 25 minutes | Cook time: 11 minutes | Serves 1

- 1 medium zucchini, diced
- 2 bacon slices
- 1 egg
- 1 tbsp coconut oil
- ½ small onion, chopped
- 1 tbsp chopped parsley
- ¼ tsp salt

1. Place the bacon in a skillet and cook for a few minutes, until crispy. Remove and set aside.
2. Warm the coconut oil and cook the onion until soft, for about 3-4 minutes, occasionally stirring. Add the zucchini, and cook for 10 more minutes until zucchini is brown and tender, but not mushy. Transfer to a plate and season with salt.
3. Crack the egg into the same skillet and fry over medium heat. Top the zucchini mixture with the bacon slices and a fried egg. Serve hot, sprinkled with parsley.

PER SERVING

Kcal: 340 | Fat: 26.8g | Net Carbs: 6.6g | Protein: 17.4g

Cheese & Aioli Eggs

Prep time: 20 minutes | Cook time: 5 minutes | Serves 8

- 8 eggs, hard-boiled, chopped
- 28 ounces tuna in brine, drained
- ½ cup lettuces, torn into pieces
- ½ cup green onions, finely chopped
- ½ cup feta cheese, crumbled
- ⅓ cup sour cream
- ½ tbsp mustard
- For Aioli:
- 1 cup mayonnaise
- 2 cloves garlic, minced
- 1 tbsp lemon juice
- Salt and black pepper, to taste

1. Set the eggs in a serving bowl. Place in tuna, onion, mustard, cheese, lettuce, and sour cream.
2. To prepare aioli, mix in a bowl mayonnaise, lemon juice, and garlic. Add in black pepper and salt. Stir in the prepared aioli to the bowl to incorporate everything. Serve with pickles.

PER SERVING

Kcal: 355 | Fat 22.5g | Net Carbs: 1.8g | Protein: 29.5g

Fontina Cheese and Chorizo Waffles

Prep time: 30 minutes | Cook time: 5 minutes | Serves 6

- 6 eggs
- 6 tbsp almond milk
- 1 tsp Spanish spice mix or allspice
- Sea salt and black pepper, to taste
- 3 chorizo sausages, cooked, chopped
- 1 cup fontina cheese, shredded

1. Using a mixing bowl, beat the eggs, Spanish spice mix, black pepper, salt, and almond milk. Add in shredded cheese and chopped sausage. Use a nonstick cooking spray to spray a waffle iron.
2. Cook the egg mixture for 5 minutes. Serve alongside homemade sugar-free tomato ketchup.

PER SERVING

Kcal: 316 | Fat: 25g | Net Carbs: 1.5g | Protein: 20.2g

Berry Green Smoothie

Prep time: 10 minutes | Cook time: 15 minutes | Serves 2

- 1 cup water
- ½ cup raspberries
- ½ cup shredded kale
- ¾ cup cream cheese
- 1 tablespoon coconut oil
- 1 scoop vanilla protein powder

1. Put the water, raspberries, kale, cream cheese, coconut oil, and protein powder in a blender and blend until smooth.
2. Pour into 2 glasses and serve immediately.

PER SERVING

Calories: 436 | Fat: 36g | Protein: 28g | Carbs: 11g | Fiber: 5g | Net Carbs: 6g

Lemon-Cashew Smoothie

Prep time: 5 minutes | Cook time: 15 minutes | Serves 1

- 1 cup unsweetened cashew milk
- ¼ cup heavy (whipping) cream
- ¼ cup freshly squeezed lemon juice
- 1 scoop plain protein powder
- 1 tablespoon coconut oil
- 1 teaspoon sweetener

1. Put the cashew milk, heavy cream, lemon juice, protein powder, coconut oil, and sweetener in a blender and blend until smooth.
2. Pour into a glass and serve immediately.

PER SERVING

Calories: 503 | Fat: 45g | Protein: 29g | Carbs: 15g | Fiber: 4g | Net Carbs: 11g

Nut Medley Granola

Prep time: 10 minute | Cook time: 1 hour | Serves 8

- 2 cups shredded unsweetened coconut
- 1 cup sliced almonds
- 1 cup raw sunflower seeds
- ½ cup raw pumpkin seeds
- ½ cup walnuts
- ½ cup melted coconut oil
- 10 drops liquid stevia
- 1 teaspoon ground cinnamon
- ½ teaspoon ground nutmeg

1. Preheat the oven to 250°F. Line 2 baking sheets with parchment paper. Set aside.
2. Toss together the shredded coconut, almonds, sunflower seeds, pumpkin seeds, and walnuts in a large bowl until mixed.
3. In a small bowl, stir together the coconut oil, stevia, cinnamon, and nutmeg until blended.
4. Pour the coconut oil mixture into the nut mixture and use your hands to blend until the nuts are very well coated.
5. Transfer the granola mixture to the baking sheets and spread it out evenly.
6. Bake the granola, stirring every 10 to 15 minutes, until the mixture is golden brown and crunchy, about 1 hour.
7. Transfer the granola to a large bowl and let the granola cool, tossing it frequently to break up the large pieces.
8. Store the granola in airtight containers in the refrigerator or freezer for up to 1 month.

PER SERVING

Calories: 391 | Fat: 38g | Protein: 10g | Carbs: 10g | Fiber: 6g | Net Carbs: 4g

Bacon-Artichoke Omelet

Prep time: 10 minutes | Cook time: 10 minutes | Serves 4

- 6 eggs, beaten
- 2 tablespoons heavy (whipping) cream
- 8 bacon slices, cooked and chopped
- 1 tablespoon olive oil
- ¼ cup chopped onion
- ½ cup chopped artichoke hearts (canned, packed in water)
- Sea salt
- Freshly ground black pepper

1. In a small bowl, whisk together the eggs, heavy cream, and bacon until well blended, and set aside.
2. Place a large skillet over medium-high heat and add the olive oil.
3. Sauté the onion until tender, about 3 minutes.
4. Pour the egg mixture into the skillet, swirling it for 1 minute.
5. Cook the omelet, lifting the edges with a spatula to let the uncooked egg flow underneath, for 2 minutes.

6. Remove from the heat, cut the omelet into quarters, and season with salt and black pepper. Transfer the omelet to plates and serve.

PER SERVING

Calories: 435 | Fat: 39g | Protein: 17g | Carbs: 5g | Fiber: 2g | Net Carbs: 3g

Sausage & Squash Omelet with Swiss Chard

Prep time: 10 minutes | Cook time: 5 minutes | Serves 1

- 2 eggs
- 1 cup Swiss chard, chopped
- 4 oz sausage, chopped
- 2 tbsp ricotta cheese
- 4 ounces roasted squash
- 1 tbsp olive oil
- Salt and black pepper, to taste
- Fresh parsley to garnish

1. Beat the eggs in a bowl, season with salt and pepper; stir in the swiss chard and the ricotta cheese.
2. In another bowl, mash the squash and add to the egg mixture. Heat ¼ tbsp of olive oil in a pan over medium heat. Add sausage and cook until browned on all sides, turning occasionally.
3. Drizzle the remaining olive oil. Pour the egg mixture over. Cook for about 2 minutes per side until the eggs are thoroughly cooked and lightly browned. Remove the pan and run a spatula around the edges of the omelet; slide it onto a warm platter. Fold in half, and serve sprinkled with fresh parsley.

PER SERVING

Kcal: 558 | Fat: 51.7g | Net Carbs: 7.5g | Protein: 32.3g

Breakfast Almond Muffins

Prep time: 30 minutes | Cook time: 20 minutes | Serves 4

- 2 drops liquid stevia
- 2 cups almond flour
- 2 tsp baking powder
- ½ tsp salt
- 8 oz cream cheese, softened
- ¼ cup melted butter
- 1 egg
- 1 cup unsweetened almond milk

1. Preheat oven to 400°F and grease a 12-cup muffin tray with cooking spray. Mix the flour, baking powder, and salt in a large bowl.
2. Bake for 20 minutes until puffy at the top and golden brown, remove to a wire rack to cool slightly for 5 minutes before serving. Serve with tea.

PER SERVING

Kcal: 320 | Fat: 30.6g | Net Carbs: 6g | Protein: 4g

Morning Almond Shake

Prep time: 4 minutes | Cook time: 5 minutes | Serves 1

- 1 ½ cups almond milk
- 2 tbsp almond butter ½ tsp almond extract
- ½ tsp cinnamon
- 2 tbsp flax meal
- 1 tbsp collagen peptides
- A pinch of salt
- 15 drops of stevia
- A handful of ice cubes

1. Add almond milk, almond butter, flax meal, almond extract, collagen peptides, a pinch of salt, and stevia to the bowl of a blender. Blitz until uniform and smooth, for about 30 seconds. Add a bit more almond milk if it's very thick.
2. Then taste, and adjust flavor as needed, adding more stevia for sweetness or almond butter to the creaminess. Pour in a smoothie glass, add the ice cubes and sprinkle with cinnamon.

PER SERVING

Kcal: 326 | Fat: 27g | Net Carbs: 6g | Protein: 19g

Duo Cheese Omelet with Pimenta and Basil

Prep time: 15 minutes | Cook time: 5 minutes | Serves 2

- 3 tbsp olive oil
- 4 eggs, beaten
- Salt and black pepper, to taste
- ¼ tsp paprika
- ¼ tsp cayenne pepper
- ½ cup asiago cheese, shredded
- ½ cup cheddar cheese, shredded
- 2 tbsp fresh basil, roughly chopped

1. Set a pan over medium heat and warm the oil. Season eggs with cayenne pepper, salt, paprika, and black pepper. Transfer to the pan and ensure they are evenly spread.
2. Top with the asiago and cheddar cheeses. Slice the omelet into two halves. Decorate with fresh basil, to serve.

PER SERVING

Kcal: 490 | Fat: 44.6g | Net Carbs: 4.5g | Protein: 22.7g

Cheese Stuffed Avocados

Prep time: 20 minutes | Cook time: 15 to 17 minutes | Serves 4

- 3 avocados, halved and pitted, skin on
- ½ cup feta cheese, crumbled
- ½ cup cheddar cheese, grated
- 2 eggs, beaten
- Salt and black pepper, to taste
- 1 tbsp fresh basil, chopped

1. Set oven to 360°F and lay the avocado halves in an ovenproof dish. In a mixing dish, mix both types of cheeses, black pepper, eggs, and salt. Split the mixture equally into the avocado halves.
2. Bake thoroughly for 15 to 17 minutes. Decorate with fresh basil before serving.

PER SERVING

Kcal: 342 | Fat: 30.4g | Net Carbs: 7.5g | Protein: 11.1g

Cauliflower & Cheese Burgers

Prep time: 35 minutes | Cook time: 20 minutes | Serves 6

- 1 ½ tbsp olive oil
- 1 onion, chopped
- 1 garlic clove, minced
- 1 pound cauliflower, grated
- 6 tbsp coconut flour
- ½ cup gruyere cheese, shredded
- 1 cup Parmesan cheese
- 2 eggs, beaten
- ½ tsp dried rosemary
- Sea salt and ground black pepper, to taste

1. Set a cast iron skillet over medium heat and warm oil. Add in garlic and onion and cook until soft, about 3 minutes. Stir in grated cauliflower and cook for a minute; allow cooling and set aside.
2. To the cooled cauliflower, add the rest of the ingredients; form balls from the mixture, then, press each ball to form burger patty.
3. Set oven to 400°F and bake the burgers for 20 minutes. Flip and bake for another 10 minutes or until the top becomes golden brown.

PER SERVING

Kcal: 416 | Fat: 33.8g | Net Carbs: 7.8g | Protein: 13g

Chapter 5
Poultry

"K.F.C." Keto Fried Chicken

Prep time: 15 minutes | Cook time: 10 minutes | Serves 8

- 1 cup vegetable oil, for frying
- 2 large eggs
- 2 tablespoons heavy whipping cream
- ⅔ cup blanched almond flour
- ⅔ cup grated Parmesan cheese
- ¼ teaspoon salt
- ½ teaspoon black pepper
- ½ teaspoon paprika
- ½ teaspoon ground cayenne
- 1 pound (approximately 4) boneless, skinless chicken thighs

1. In a medium pot over medium heat add vegetable oil. Make sure it is about 1" deep. Heat oil to 350°F, frequently monitoring to maintain the temperature by adjusting heat during frying.
2. In a medium bowl, add eggs and heavy whipping cream. Beat until well mixed.
3. In a separate medium bowl, add almond flour, Parmesan cheese, salt, pepper, paprika, and cayenne and mix.
4. Cut each thigh into two even pieces. If wet, pat dry.
5. Coat each piece first in the dry breading, then in the egg wash, and then the breading again.
6. Shake off any excess breading and lower the chicken into the hot oil. Fry until deep brown and cooked through, about 3–5 minutes on each side, and then drain on paper towels.
7. Repeat until all chicken is cooked. Serve right away while hot and crispy.

PER SERVING

Calories: 470 | Fat: 34g | Protein: 31g | Sodium: 507mg| Fiber: 2g |Carbohydrates: 5g | Net Carbs: 3g | Sugar: 1g

Alex's "Chick And Brock" Casserole

Prep time: 10 minutes | Cook time: 50 minutes | Serves 8

- 1 cup heavy whipping cream
- 1 cup mascarpone cheese, softened
- 1 cup grated Parmesan cheese
- 3 cloves garlic, peeled and minced
- 2 teaspoons dried parsley
- ½ teaspoon salt
- ½ teaspoon black pepper
- ½ teaspoon garlic salt
- 1 pound cooked, shredded boneless chicken breast
- 4 cups raw broccoli florets
- 2 cups shredded whole milk mozzarella cheese, divided

1. Preheat oven to 375°F. Grease a 9" × 12" casserole dish.
2. In a large bowl, add all ingredients except chicken, broccoli, and mozzarella. Mix until blended to thick sauce.
3. In a separate large bowl, mix shredded chicken, broccoli, and 1 cup mozzarella. Add sauce mixture and mix well.
4. Transfer to casserole dish. Spread remaining 1 cup mozzarella evenly over top.
5. Bake 40–50 minutes or until broccoli is tender and cheese is golden brown.

PER SERVING

Calories: 427 | Fat: 23g | Protein: 31g | Sodium: 740mg| Fiber: 1g |Carbohydrates: 9g | Net Carbs: 8g | Sugar: 3g

Merry Christmas Chicken

Prep time: 10 minutes | Cook time: 23 minutes | Serves 4

- 4 (4.2-ounce) boneless, skinless chicken breasts
- 1 medium red bell pepper, seeded and chopped
- 1 medium green bell pepper, seeded and chopped
- 4 ounces full-fat cream cheese, softened
- ¼ teaspoon salt
- ¼ teaspoon black pepper
- ¼ teaspoon paprika
- ¼ teaspoon dried parsley
- Preheat oven to 375°F.

1. Place wax paper on both sides of chicken breasts. Use a rolling pin, kitchen mallet, or cast iron skillet to pound chicken until thin (less than ¼").
2. In a medium microwave-safe bowl, microwave bell peppers 3 minutes.
3. In a separate medium bowl, mix cream cheese and softened bell peppers. Add salt and pepper.
4. Cover a large baking sheet with foil. Coat evenly with cooking spray. Lay flattened breasts on baking sheet.
5. Place one-quarter of the cream cheese mixture into the center of each pounded chicken and roll. Secure with a wet toothpick.
6. Garnish chicken with paprika and parsley to continue Christmas theme.
7. Bake 20 minutes. Serve warm.

PER SERVING

Calories: 240 | Fat: 11g | Protein: 28g | Sodium: 294mg| Fiber: 1g |Carbohydrates: 5g | Net Carbs: 4g | Sugar: 3g

Stuffed Chicken For Suppah

Prep time: 10 minutes | Cook time: 24 minutes | Serves 1

- 6 ounces chopped fresh spinach
- 2 cloves garlic, peeled and minced
- 1½ cups crumbled feta cheese, divided
- 4 (4.8-ounce) boneless, skinless chicken breasts
- 2 medium Roma tomatoes, each sliced into 8 rounds

1. Preheat oven to 450°F. Line a baking sheet with parchment paper or greased foil.
2. Steam spinach in microwave 2–3 minutes (or cook in a medium skillet 3–5 minutes over medium heat). Let cooked spinach cool, then squeeze out excess moisture.
3. To a medium bowl, add spinach, garlic, and ¾ cup feta cheese.
4. Microwave cream cheese to soften for 15–30 seconds. Add to spinach mixture, stirring thoroughly.
5. Place chicken on baking sheet. Cut horizontal slit in each breast, creating a pocket. (Center your cut midway, between top and bottom of the breast.)
6. Stuff each breast with one-quarter of the total spinach mixture. Sprinkle lightly with pepper.
7. Top each breast with four tomato slices and remaining feta.
8. Bake 16–20 minutes until chicken is thoroughly cooked. Tent pan with foil if cheese starts to brown before chicken is done.

PER SERVING

Calories: 364 | Fat: 19g | Protein: 40g | Sodium: 654mg|
Fiber: 2g |Carbohydrates: 7g | Net Carbs: 5g | Sugar: 4g

Fluffy Chicken

Prep time: 15 minutes | Cook time: 10 minutes | Serves 8

- ½ cup chicken broth
- 1 (1-ounce) package ranch powder seasoning mix
- 2 pounds boneless, skinless chicken breasts
- 8 ounces full-fat cream cheese, softened
- 8 slices no-sugar-added bacon, cooked and crumbled
- ½ cup shredded Cheddar cheese

1. Add chicken broth to slow cooker and stir in ranch powder seasoning packet.
2. Remove lid. Drain excess broth, leaving around ½ cup for moisture depending on preference.
3. Shred chicken.
4. In a small microwave-safe bowl, microwave cream cheese 20–30 seconds. Combine with crumbled bacon and Cheddar cheese.
5. Add cream cheese mixture to shredded chicken. Cover and heat 10 minutes on high temperature until cheeses melt. Serve warm.

PER SERVING

Calories: 325 | Fat: 16g | Protein: 33g | Sodium: 716mg|Fiber:
|Carbohydrates: 3g | Net Carbs: 3g | Sugar: 1g

Indoor Bbq Chicken

Prep time: 10 minutes | Cook time: 45 minutes | Serves 4

- 1 tablespoon sriracha sauce
- 2 teaspoons chili powder
- 2 teaspoons garlic powder
- 2 teaspoons onion powder
- 1 tablespoon apple cider vinegar
- 1 tablespoon paprika
- 1 (1-gram) packet 0g net carb sweetener
- ½ teaspoon xanthan gum
- 1 cup crushed tomatoes
- 4 medium chicken thighs with skin

1. Preheat oven to 375°F. Line a baking sheet with parchment paper or greased foil.
2. In a small saucepan over medium-high heat, make the barbecue sauce by mixing all the ingredients except the chicken and bring to boil. Let simmer 5 minutes, stirring regularly.
3. Using a basting brush, apply about half the barbecue sauce to both sides of thighs. Place chicken on baking sheet.
4. Cook 20 minutes. Flip chicken and reapply remaining sauce. Cook another 20 minutes until chicken is thoroughly cooked.
5. Serve warm or cold.

PER SERVING

Calories: 362 | Fat: 19g | Protein: 34g | Sodium: 951mg|
Fiber: 3g |Carbohydrates: 10g | Net Carbs: 7g | Sugar: 4g

Yippee Chicken Gyros

Prep time: 15 minutes | Cook time: 15 minutes | Serves 4

- 1 tablespoon olive oil
- 4 (3-ounce) boneless, skinless chicken thighs, cut into ½" strips
- ¼ teaspoon garlic powder
- ⅛ teaspoon ground black pepper
- 4 pieces low-carb Flatbread (double the Phony Philly Cheesesteak recipe in this chapter)
- ½ cup full-fat sour cream
- 1 teaspoon Greek seasoning
- 1½ cups Pedestrian Mediterranean Salad

1. In a medium saucepan over medium heat, heat oil. Add chicken, garlic powder, and pepper. Cook 12–15 minutes, stirring regularly.
2. Set out four plates with a Flatbread on each.
3. Divide chicken evenly on Flatbreads. Top evenly with equal amounts Pedestrian Mediterranean Salad and sour cream mixture.
4. Serve immediately. Eat gyro folded over as you would a taco.

PER SERVING

Calories: 957 | Fat: 74g | Protein: 48g | Sodium:
1458mg| Fiber: 6g |Carbohydrates: 16g | Net Carbs: 10g
| Sugar: 5g | Sugar Alcohol: 0g

Buffet Line Butter Chicken

Prep time: 15 minutes | Cook time: 25 minutes | Serves 4

- 1 pound boneless, skinless chicken breasts, cut into 1" cubes
- 2 tablespoons olive oil, divided
- 2 tablespoons garam masala
- 2 teaspoons grated fresh ginger
- 2 teaspoons garlic powder
- ⅛ teaspoon salt
- ⅛ teaspoon ground black pepper
- 1½ cups vegetable broth
- ¼ cup 100% tomato sauce
- ¼ cup heavy whipping cream

1. Add chicken and 1 tablespoon oil to a large (2-gallon) resealable bag. Squeeze air out of bag and seal. Knead bag until all chicken is coated. Add garam masala, ginger, garlic powder, salt, and pepper to bag and seal as before. Knead bag again until all chicken is coated. Let marinate in refrigerator at least 1 hour, preferably overnight.
2. In a large skillet over medium heat, heat remaining 1 tablespoon oil. Add chicken and marinade and sauté 5 minutes while stirring.
3. Stir in broth and cook 15 minutes, stirring regularly. Stir in tomato sauce and cream and simmer 3–5 minutes until thickened to desired consistency.
4. Serve warm over your favorite naan or rice substitute.

PER SERVING

Calories: 261 | Fat: 15g | Protein: 27g | Sodium: 641mg| Fiber: 0g |Carbohydrates: 5g | Net Carbs: 5g | Sugar: 2g | Sugar Alcohol: 0g

Orange Crush Chicken

Prep time: 10 minutes | Cook time: 3 hours | Serves 2

- 1 pound boneless, skinless chicken thighs
- ½ medium white onion, peeled and sliced into wedges
- ¼ cup no-sugar-added ketchup
- 12 ounces Diet Orange Crush soda
- ⅓ cup 0g net carbs sweetener
- 2 cups chopped (1" chunks) red and green bell pepper

1. Add all ingredients except bell peppers to a slow cooker and stir to blend. Cook on high 2 hours, 30 minutes.
2. Add bell peppers to slow cooker. Continue cooking 30 minutes on high.
3. Let cool and evenly divide into two bowls. Serve warm.

PER SERVING

Calories: 379 | Fat: 14g | Protein: 41g | Sodium: 502mg| Fiber: 3g |Carbohydrates: 29g | Net Carbs: 10g | Sugar: 9g | Sugar Alcohol: 16g

Silky Chicken with Mushroom Sauce

Prep time: 10 minutes | Cook time: 20 minutes | Serves 4

- 4 (4.2-ounce) boneless, skinless chicken breasts
- 4 tablespoons olive oil, divided
- 2 cups sliced mushrooms
- ½ cup diced onion
- 2 tablespoons unblanched almond flour
- 1 clove garlic, peeled and minced
- ½ cup half and half, divided
- 2 tablespoons chopped dried thyme
- ¼ teaspoon salt
- ¼ teaspoon black pepper
- Pound chicken breasts to even thickness, about ¼" thick.

1. In a large sauté pan over medium heat, heat 2 tablespoons olive oil and then add chicken. Cook 1–2 minutes until brown on each side. Reduce heat to low.
2. Cover with secure lid and let cook additional 15 minutes (flipping at 7½ minutes). After 15 minutes, remove chicken from pan, and cover to keep warm.
3. In same pan, add mushrooms, 2 tablespoons oil, and onion. Cook over medium heat 10–15 minutes, stirring regularly. Stir in almond flour to thicken and cook an additional 2–3 minutes.
4. Add garlic, ¼ cup half and half, thyme, salt, and pepper. Keep stirring, adding more half and half if needed until the desired consistency is achieved.
5. Serve warm chicken on a plate topped with mushroom sauce.

PER SERVING

Calories: 327 | Fat: 20g | Protein: 29g | Sodium: 205mg| Fiber: 2g |Carbohydrates: 7g | Net Carbs: 5g | Sugar: 3g

Drunken Pot Roast

Prep time: 5 minutes | Cook time: 8 hours | Serves 8

- 1 (4-pound) roast
- 1 (1-ounce) package ranch dressing mix
- 1 cup chopped celery
- ½ cup unsalted butter, softened
- 1 (12-ounce) can low-carb beer

1. Place roast in slow cooker and cover with dressing mix, celery, butter, and beer.
2. Cover and cook on low heat for 8 hours.
3. After cooking is finished, let roast sit 15 minutes. Carve and serve warm.

PER SERVING

Calories: 556 | Fat: 34g | Protein: 49g | Sodium: 446mg| Fiber: 0g |Carbohydrates: 4g | Net Carbs: 4g | Sugar: 0g

Chicken Wings with Orange Ginger Sauce

Prep time: 5 minutes | Cook time: 40 minutes | Serves 4

FOR THE WINGS

- 2 pounds chicken wings
- 2 tablespoons coconut oil, melted
- For The Sauce
- 4 tablespoons grass-fed butter
- 2 teaspoons grated fresh ginger
- 2 teaspoons minced garlic
- Zest and juice of 1 orange
- 2 tablespoons monk fruit sweetener, granulated form
- To Make The Wings

1. Preheat the oven. Set the oven temperature to 400°F. Line a baking sheet with parchment paper.
2. Prepare the wings. In a large bowl, toss the wings with the coconut oil and spread them on the baking sheet.
3. Bake the wings. Bake the wings for 20 minutes, turn them over, and bake them for another 20 minutes until they're golden and cooked through (165°F internal temperature).

TO MAKE THE SAUCE

4. Make the sauce. While the chicken wings are baking, put a small saucepan over medium-high heat and melt the butter. Add the ginger and garlic and sauté for 3 minutes. Stir in the orange zest, orange juice, and monk fruit sweetener and bring the sauce to a boil. Reduce the heat to medium and simmer, stirring from time to time, until the sauce gets thick and shiny, 10 to 15 minutes.
5. Glaze the wings. Transfer the wings to a large bowl and pour in the sauce, tossing the wings to coat them completely. Serve with lots of napkins.

PER SERVING

Calories: 674 | Total Fat: 54g | Total Carbs: 3g | Fiber: 0g | Net Carbs: 3g | Sodium: 274mg | Protein: 42g

N'Awlins Chicken

Prep time: 10 minutes | Cook time: 41 minutes | Serves 6

- 1 teaspoon olive oil
- 2 pounds boneless, skinless chicken thighs
- ¼ teaspoon salt
- ⅛ teaspoon black pepper
- 3 tablespoons unsalted butter
- ¼ cup minced onion
- 3 cloves garlic, peeled and minced
- 1 cup bourbon
- 2 cups chicken stock

1. In a large saucepan over medium heat, heat olive oil, then add chicken thighs. Season with salt and pepper and sear 3 minutes on each side until golden brown.
2. Add butter, onion, and garlic, and sauté until the onion and garlic are brown (3–5 minutes).
3. Pour bourbon and chicken stock over chicken and boil.
4. Reduce heat to medium and cook 25–30 minutes, flipping chicken halfway through.
5. Cool and serve chicken with bourbon sauce.

PER SERVING

Calories: 391 | Fat: 18g | Protein: 40g | Sodium: 372mg| Fiber: 0g |Carbohydrates: 4g | Net Carbs: 4g | Sugar: 2g

Dancing Drunken Chicken

Prep time: 10 minutes | Cook time: 60 minutes | Serves 4

- 2 teaspoons salt
- ½ teaspoon ground black pepper
- 1½ teaspoons poultry seasoning
- 1 (3½-pound) whole chicken
- 2 tablespoons olive oil
- 1 (12-ounce) can low-carb beer

1. Preheat outdoor grill over medium heat. Line a small baking sheet with foil.
2. In a small bowl, combine salt, black pepper, and poultry seasoning.
3. Brush exterior of chicken with oil and rub seasonings over exterior as well as interior of chicken.
4. Open beer and take a nice-sized swig, at least 1 ounce. Stand beer on the prepared baking sheet and slide the whole chicken completely over the can.
5. Move the baking sheet to the grill and cook chicken with the lid down 45–60 minutes until internal temperature is at least 165°F.
6. Remove from the grill. When cool enough to handle, cut and serve.

PER SERVING

Calories: 505 | Fat: 32g | Protein: 42g | Sodium: 12761mg| Fiber: 0g |Carbohydrates: 1g | Net Carbs: 1g | Sugar: 0g | Sugar Alcohol: 0g

Chipotle Chicken Fajita Bowl

Prep time: 10 minutes | Cook time: 30 minutes | Serves 4

- 3 tablespoons unsalted butter
- 1½ pounds boneless, skinless chicken thighs, cut into thin strips
- ¼ teaspoon salt
- 1 small yellow onion, peeled and diced
- 1 large green bell pepper, seeded and diced
- 2 tablespoons taco seasoning
- 6 cups chopped romaine lettuce
- 1 cup shredded Mexican cheese
- ½ cup full-fat sour cream
- 2 large avocados, peeled, pitted, and diced
- 1 small tomato, chopped
- 4 tablespoons finely chopped cilantro

1. In a large skillet over medium heat, add butter and fry chicken for 5 minutes while stirring just to brown. Season chicken with salt. Sauté 10–15 minutes, stirring regularly.
2. Add onion, bell pepper, and taco seasoning. Reduce heat to low and cook 7–10 minutes. Stir often until vegetables have softened.
3. Distribute lettuce evenly to serving bowls, then add cooked chicken and vegetables. Top with cheese, sour cream, diced avocados, tomato, and cilantro.

PER SERVING

Calories: 610 | Fat: 40g | Protein: 39g | Sodium: 660mg| Fiber: 8g |Carbohydrates: 16g | Net Carbs: 8g | Sugar: 5g

Four Horsemen Butter Chicken

Prep time: 10 minutes | Cook time: 27 minutes | Serves 8

- 1 tablespoon unsalted butter
- 1 tablespoon olive oil
- 1 medium onion, peeled and diced
- 3 cloves garlic, peeled and minced
- 2 teaspoons peeled and grated fresh ginger
- 2 pounds boneless, skinless chicken breasts, cooked and cut into ¾" chunks
- 3 ounces tomato paste
- 3 ounces red curry paste
- 1 tablespoon garam masala
- 1 teaspoon chili powder
- 1 teaspoon mustard seeds
- 1 teaspoon ground coriander
- 1 teaspoon curry
- 1 teaspoon salt
- ⅛ teaspoon black pepper
- 1 (14-ounce) can unsweetened coconut milk
- 1 teaspoon chopped cilantro

1. In a large skillet over medium-high heat, heat butter and olive oil. Add onion and fry until soft, about 3–5 minutes. Mix in garlic and ginger. Cook 1–2 minutes more.
2. Add cooked chicken to skillet. Add tomato paste, red curry paste, garam masala, chili powder, mustard seeds, coriander, and curry. Add salt and pepper. Stir until well mixed and chicken cubes are well coated.
3. Stir in coconut milk and bring to boil. Reduce heat. Cover and simmer 20 minutes.
4. Remove from heat. Let cool 10 minutes and serve warm with cilantro sprinkled on top.

PER SERVING

Calories: 298 | Fat: 16g | Protein: 30g | Sodium: 729mg| Fiber: 1g |Carbohydrates: 8g | Net Carbs: 7g | Sugar: 2g

Inferno Tandoori Chicken

Prep time: 60 minutes | Cook time: 45 minutes | Serves 4

- 2 teaspoons paprika
- 2 teaspoons ginger paste
- 1 teaspoon ground coriander
- 1 teaspoon ground cumin
- 1 teaspoon garam masala
- 1 teaspoon ground cayenne
- 1 cup plain whole milk Greek yogurt
- 4 (4.2-ounce) boneless, skinless chicken breasts

1. In a medium bowl, mix together all spices. Add yogurt, stirring to blend thoroughly.
2. Using a spatula, scoop yogurt mixture into a gallon-sized Ziploc bag.
3. Cut each chicken breast into four strips.
4. Transfer chicken to marinate in yogurt mixture, sealing bag and carefully kneading through the plastic bag, ensuring chicken is completely covered with sauce.
5. Let sit in refrigerator for at least 1 hour (but preferably overnight).
6. Preheat oven to 400°F. Line a baking sheet with parchment paper.
7. Remove chicken pieces from the bag and place onto baking sheet, trying to keep as much of the sauce as possible that clings to the meat. Don't add any extra sauce from the bag. Bake 40–45 minutes or until fully cooked, flipping once at 20 minutes.
8. Remove from the oven and serve warm.

PER SERVING

Calories: 189 | Fat: 5g | Protein: 33g | Sodium: 65mg| Fiber: 1g |Carbohydrates: 3g | Net Carbs: 2g | Sugar: 2g

Turkey Taco Boats

Prep time: 10 minutes | Cook time: 30 minutes | Serves 4

- 1 pound lean ground turkey
- 1 (1-ounce) package taco seasoning
- ¾ cup water
- ½ small onion, peeled and finely chopped
- ½ large green bell pepper, seeded and chopped
- 1 (4-ounce) can tomato sauce
- 8 large romaine lettuce leaves
- 1 small tomato, diced

1. In a medium pan over medium heat, brown turkey. (There shouldn't be any fat to drain.) Stir in seasoning packet and water.
2. Add onion, bell pepper, and tomato sauce to meat and stir. Cover and reduce heat to low for 15 minutes.
3. Add two lettuce "boats" per plate and fill one-eighth of the meat mixture into each boat.
4. Top with fresh tomato and serve.

PER SERVING

Calories: 220 | Fat: 9g | Protein: 23g | Sodium: 728mg| Fiber: 3g |Carbohydrates: 10g | Net Carbs: 7g | Sugar: 4g

Verde Chicken Enchiladas

Prep time: 20 minutes | Cook time: 20 minutes | Serves 8

- 2 (4.2-ounce) boneless, skinless chicken breasts, cooked
- ½ cup cooked, diced mushrooms
- ½ cup cooked, diced zucchini
- 8 small low-carb flour tortillas
- 1 cup green enchilada sauce
- 1 cup shredded Cheddar cheese
- 1 medium green onion, finely chopped
- ¼ cup freshly minced cilantro, divided
- ¼ cup sliced black olives
- ⅓ cup full-fat sour cream

1. Preheat oven to 350°F. Grease a 9" × 9" baking dish.
2. In a medium bowl, finely shred cooked chicken breasts. Add mushrooms and zucchini and stir to combine.
3. On a large baking sheet or clean cutting board, lay out tortillas one at a time and evenly distribute chicken and vegetable mixture in center of each tortilla. Roll each tortilla over chicken and vegetables to make tight rolls.
4. Put rolls in baking dish. Cover with green enchilada sauce and evenly top with cheese, green onion, half of the cilantro, and olives.
5. Bake 15–20 minutes until cheese melts.
6. Let cool 10 minutes. Top with sour cream and remaining cilantro and serve.

PER SERVING

Calories: 200 | Fat: 10g | Protein: 15g | Sodium: 529mg| Fiber: 9g |Carbohydrates: 18g | Net Carbs: 9g | Sugar: 2g

White Wine Seared Chicken Breasts

Prep time: 5 minutes | Cook time: 15 minutes | Serves 4

- 4 medium boneless, skinless chicken breasts (8 ounces each)
- 1 teaspoon sea salt
- ¼ teaspoon black pepper
- 4 tablespoons (½ stick) butter, cut into 1- tablespoon pats
- 2 cloves garlic, minced
- 1 medium (2.5-ounce) shallot, finely chopped
- ½ cup white cooking wine
- ½ cup chicken broth
- ½ tablespoon chopped fresh parsley
- ½ tablespoon fresh thyme, chopped

1. Season the chicken on both sides with sea salt and black pepper.
2. In a large skillet or sauté pan, melt 1 tablespoon of the butter over medium-high heat. Add the chicken and sauté for 5 to 8 minutes per side, until cooked through and browned.
3. Remove the chicken from the pan and cover with foil.
4. Add another 1 tablespoon butter to the pan. Add the garlic and shallot, and sauté for about 1 minute, until fragrant.
5. Add the wine and broth to the pan and use a wooden spoon to scrape any browned bits from the bottom. Bring to a gentle boil, then lower the heat and simmer for about 7 to 8 minutes, until the liquid volume is reduced by half.
6. Reduce the heat to low. Stir in the remaining 2 tablespoons butter, parsley, and thyme, just until the butter melts.
7. Serve the sauce over the chicken.

PER SERVING

Calories: 288 | Fat: 14g | Total Carbs: 2g | Net Carbs: 2g | Protein: 29g

Bacon-Wrapped Chicken Thighs

Prep time: 5 minutes | Cook time: 15 minutes | Serves 4

- 8 medium boneless, skinless chicken thighs (~2.5 ounces each)
- ¼ cup avocado oil
- ½ teaspoon paprika
- 1 teaspoon sea salt
- ¼ teaspoon black pepper
- 8 slices bacon

1. Preheat the oven to 450°F. Line a sheet pan with foil.
2. Place the chicken thighs in a single layer on the baking sheet so that they don't touch each other.
3. Brush the chicken on both sides with the oil. Season with paprika, sea salt, and black pepper.
4. Wrap each chicken thigh tightly in a slice of bacon, tucking the end underneath to secure it. Place seam side down on the baking sheet.
5. Roast for 18 to 22 minutes, until the chicken is almost or just barely cooked through. Remove from the oven and drain any liquid from the pan.
6. Move the oven rack to the top. Switch the oven to broil and place the chicken under the broiler for 2 to 3 minutes, until the bacon is crispy.

PER SERVING

Calories: 606 | Fat: 52g | Total Carbs: 0g | Net Carbs: 0g | Protein: 30g

Slow Cooker Creamy Salsa Chicken

Prep time: 5 minutes | Cook time: 15 minutes | Serves 4

- 4 boneless, skinless chicken breasts (6 ounces each)
- 1 cup Pantry Staple Salsa
- 3 ounces (6 tablespoons) cream cheese
- 1 cup (4 ounces) shredded pepper jack cheese

1. Place the chicken breasts in a slow cooker and pour the salsa over them. Cook on low for 6 to 8 hours or on high for 3 to 4 hours, until the chicken is cooked through and tender.
2. Close to serving time, heat the cream cheese in the microwave for about 30 seconds, or let it sit at room temperature to soften.
3. Remove the chicken from the slow cooker and set aside, scraping any excess salsa to leave it in the slow cooker. Whisk the cream cheese in the slow cooker until the sauce is smooth.
4. Return the chicken to the slow cooker and sprinkle the pepper jack over it. Cover and keep the heat on for 10 to 15 minutes, until the cheese melts.
5. Spoon the creamy salsa mixture over the chicken to serve.

PER SERVING

Calories: 350 | Fat: 18g | Total Carbs: 5g | Net Carbs: 5g | Protein: 36g

Crispy Orange Chicken

Prep time: 5 minutes | Cook time: 15 minutes | Serves 4

CHICKEN:

- 1 pound boneless, skinless chicken breast, cut into 1-inch pieces
- ½ teaspoon sea salt
- ¼ teaspoon black pepper
- 2 large eggs
- 3 ounces pork rinds, crushed to the texture of breadcrumbs
- 2 tablespoons avocado oil
- Orange Sauce:
- 1 tablespoon avocado oil
- 2 cloves garlic, minced
- ½ cup coconut aminos
- ¼ cup white wine vinegar
- 2 tablespoons orange zest
- 2 tablespoons (0.6 ounce) powdered erythritol
- ½ teaspoon ground ginger

PREPARE THE CHICKEN:

1. Season the chicken with sea salt and black pepper.
2. In a small bowl, whisk the eggs. In a medium bowl, place the crushed pork rinds.
3. In a large skillet, heat the oil over medium-high heat.
4. Dip the chicken pieces in the egg, shake off the excess, then coat with the pork rind crumbs on all sides. (Alternatively, you can place all the chicken pieces in the egg at once, and take them out one by one to dip in the crumbs.) Working in batches, place a single layer of chicken into the pan. Cook for a few minutes on each side, until golden and cooked through.
5. Remove the chicken from the pan and cover with foil to keep warm. Repeat with the remaining chicken pieces. Keep the skillet for the sauce.

MAKE THE ORANGE SAUCE:

1. While the chicken rests, in the same skillet, heat the oil over medium heat. Add the garlic and sauté for about 1 minute, until fragrant.
2. Add the coconut aminos, wine vinegar, orange zest, powdered erythritol, and ground ginger. Use a wooden spoon to scrape any browned bits from the bottom and deglaze the pan.
3. Bring the sauce to a gentle boil, reduce the heat, and simmer for 8 to 10 minutes, until the volume is reduced, and the sauce thickens and looks glossy.
4. Return the chicken to the pan and toss to coat. The sauce will thicken as it cools from hot to warm.

PER SERVING

Calories: 328 | Fat: 18g | Total Carbs: 12g | Net Carbs: 7g | Protein: 29g

Chili-Lime Turkey Burgers

Prep time: 5 minutes | Cook time: 15 minutes | Serves 4

- 1 pound ground turkey
- 3 tablespoons 2-Minute Avocado Oil Mayonnaise
- 1 teaspoon lime zest
- 1 teaspoon lime juice
- 1 tablespoon chili powder
- ¾ teaspoon sea salt
- ½ teaspoon dried oregano
- ¼ teaspoon garlic powder
- ⅛ teaspoon cayenne pepper (optional)
- 1 tablespoon avocado oil

1. In a large bowl, combine all the ingredients except the avocado oil. Use your hands to mix, being careful not to overmix.
2. Divide the meat into 4 portions and form into patties, ⅓ to ½ inch thick. Make a thumbprint in each.
3. In a sauté pan, heat the oil over medium to medium-high heat. Cook the burgers for 4 to 5 minutes per side, until cooked through.

PER SERVING

Calories: 283 | Fat: 21g | Total Carbs: 1g | Net Carbs: 1g | Protein: 21g

Caprese Chicken Thighs

Prep time: 5 minutes | Cook time: 15 minutes | Serves 4

- ⅓ cup olive oil
- 3 tablespoons balsamic vinegar, divided into 2 tablespoons and 1 tablespoon
- 1 teaspoon Italian seasoning
- ½ teaspoon garlic powder
- ½ teaspoon sea salt
- ¼ teaspoon black pepper
- 8 boneless, skinless chicken thighs (~2.5 ounces each)
- 4 ounces fresh mozzarella cheese, cut into 8 slices (0.5 ounce each)
- 2 medium Roma (plum) tomatoes, thinly sliced
- 2 tablespoons fresh basil, cut into ribbons

1. In a large bowl, whisk together the oil, 2 tablespoons of balsamic vinegar, the Italian seasoning, garlic powder, sea salt, and black pepper.
2. Add the chicken thighs and push down into the marinade. Set aside for 20 minutes, or refrigerate until ready to use.
3. Meanwhile, preheat the oven to 375°F. Line a sheet pan with foil or parchment paper.
4. Shake off any excess marinade from each piece of chicken and arrange on the baking sheet in a single layer without touching.
5. Top each chicken thigh with a slice of mozzarella, covering most of it. You may need to cut a piece in half to cover the chicken better. Place 2 slices of tomato on top of the mozzarella.
6. Roast for 23 to 28 minutes, until the chicken is cooked through. You may need to pour off extra liquid from the pan at the end.
7. Drizzle the chicken with the remaining 1 tablespoon balsamic vinegar (or with a reduction by simmering more balsamic vinegar in a small saucepan). Garnish with basil ribbons.

PER SERVING

Calories: 564 | Fat: 46g | Total Carbs: 4g | Net Carbs: 4g | Protein: 31g

Chapter 6
Pork, Beef & Lamb

Weekend Spicy Burgers with Sweet Onion

Prep time: 20 minutes | Cook time: 10 minutes | Serves 6

- 2 lb ground pork
- Pink salt and chili pepper to taste
- 3 tbsp olive oil
- 1 tbsp butter
- 1 white onion, sliced into rings
- 1 tbsp balsamic vinegar
- 3 drops liquid stevia
- 6 low carb burger buns, halved
- 2 firm tomatoes, sliced into rings

1. Combine the pork, salt and chili pepper in a bowl, and mold out 6 patties.
2. Heat the olive oil in a skillet over medium heat, and fry the patties for 4 to 5 minutes on each side until golden brown on the outside. Remove onto a plate, and sit for 3 minutes.
3. Melt butter in a skillet over medium heat, sauté onions for 2 minutes, and stir in the balsamic vinegar and liquid stevia. Cook for 30 seconds stirring once, or twice until caramelized. In each bun, place a patty, top with some onion rings and 2 tomato rings.
4. Serve the burgers with cheddar cheese dip.

PER SERVING

Cal: 315 | Net Carbs: 6g | Fat: 23g | Protein 16g

Green Pork Bake

Prep time: 45 minutes | Cook time: 40 minutes |Serves 4

- 1 pound ground pork
- 1 onion, chopped
- 1 garlic clove, minced
- ½ green beans, chopped
- Salt and black pepper to taste
- 1 zucchini, sliced
- ¼ cup heavy cream
- 5 eggs
- ½ cup Monterey Jack cheese, grated

1. In a bowl, mix onion, green beans, ground pork, garlic, black pepper and salt. Layer the meat mixture on the bottom of a small greased baking dish. Spread zucchini slices on top.
2. In a separate bowl, combine cheese, eggs and heavy cream. Top with this creamy mixture and bake for 40 minutes at 360 F, until the edges and top become brown.

PER SERVING

Cal: 335 | Fat 21.3g | Net Carbs: 3.9g | Protein 27.7g

Pork Chops with Basil Tomato Sauce

Prep time: 50 minutes | Cook time: 34 minutes |Serves 4

- 4 pork chops
- ½ tbsp fresh basil, chopped
- 1 garlic clove, minced
- 1 tbsp olive oil
- 7 ounces canned diced tomatoes
- ½ tbsp tomato paste
- Salt and black pepper, to taste
- ½ red chili, finely chopped

1. Season the pork with salt and black pepper. Set a pan over medium heat and warm oil, place in the pork chops, cook for 3 minutes, turn and cook for another 3 minutes; remove to a bowl. Add in the garlic and cook for 30 seconds.
2. Stir in the tomato paste, tomatoes, and chili; bring to a boil, and reduce heat to medium-low. Place in the pork chops, cover the pan and simmer everything for 30 minutes. Remove the pork chops to plates and sprinkle with fresh oregano to serve.

PER SERVING

Cal: 425 | Fat: 25g | Net Carbs: 2.5g | Protein 39g

Tender Pork Loin Steaks with Mustard Sauce

Prep time: 15 minutes | Cook time: 13 minutes |Serves 2

- ½ tbsp butter
- ½ tbsp olive oil
- 4 pork loin chops
- ½ tsp Dijon mustard
- ½ tbsp soy sauce
- ½ tsp lemon juice
- 2 tsp cumin seeds
- ½ tbsp water
- Salt and black pepper, to taste
- ½ cup chives, chopped

1. Set a pan over medium heat and warm butter and olive oil, add in the pork chops, season with salt, and pepper, cook for 4 minutes, turn and cook for additional 4 minutes. Remove to a plate.
2. In a bowl, mix the water with lemon juice, cumin seeds, mustard and soy sauce. Pour the mustard sauce in the same pan and simmer for 5 minutes. Spread over pork, top with chives and serve.

PER SERVING

Cal: 382 | Fat: 21.5g | Net Carbs: 1.2g | Protein 38g

Caramelized Onion over Pork Burgers

Prep time: 20 minutes | Cook time: 10 minutes |Serves 4

- 2 tbsp olive oil
- 1 pound ground pork
- Salt and black pepper to taste
- ½ tsp chili pepper
- 1 tbsp parsley
- ½ tbsp balsamic vinegar
- 1 drop liquid stevia
- 1 tomato, sliced into rings
- 1 tbsp mayonnaise

1. Warm half of the oil in a skillet over medium heat, sauté onions for 2 minutes, and stir in the balsamic vinegar and liquid stevia. Cook for 30 seconds stirring once or twice until caramelized; remove to a plate. Combine the pork, salt, black pepper and chili pepper in a bowl, and mold out 2 patties.
2. Heat the remaining olive oil in a skillet over medium heat and fry the patties for 4 to 5 minutes on each side until golden brown on the outside. Remove to a plate and sit for 3 minutes.
3. In each tomato slice, place half of the mayonnaise and a patty, and top with some onion rings. Cover with another tomato slice and serve.

PER SERVING

Cal: 510 | Fat: 41.2g | Net Carbs: 2.6g | Protein 31g

Baked Winter Pork Stew

Prep time: 40 minutes | Cook time: 40 minutes |Serves 4

- 3 tsp olive oil
- 1 pound ground pork
- 1 cup vegetable stock
- 14 oz canned tomatoes with juice
- 1 carrot, chopped
- 1 celery stick, chopped
- 1 lb butternut squash, chopped
- 1 tbsp Worcestershire sauce
- 2 bay leaves
- Salt and black pepper to taste
- 3 tbsp fresh parsley, chopped
- 1 onion, chopped
- 1 tsp dried sage
- 1 garlic clove, minced

1. Preheat oven to 360 F.
2. Warm olive oil over medium heat and add the onion, garlic, celery, carrot, and ground pork.
3. Cook for 10 minutes, stirring often until no longer pink.
4. Adjust the seasonings.
5. Remove and discard the bay leaves and transfer to a baling casserole. Bake in the oven for 10 minutes until the top is golden brown. Serve sprinkled with parsley.

PER SERVING

Cal: 353 | Fat: 16.5g | Net Carbs: 6.6g | Protein 26.1g

Beef Steaks with Creamy Bacon & Mushrooms

Prep time: 50 minutes | Cook time: 40 minutes |Serves 4

- 2 oz bacon, chopped
- 1 cup mushrooms, sliced
- 1 garlic clove, chopped
- 1 shallot, chopped
- 1 cup heavy cream
- 1 pound beef steaks
- 1 tsp ground nutmeg
- Salt and black pepper to taste
- 1 tbsp parsley, chopped

1. In a frying pan over medium heat, cook the bacon for 2-3 minutes and set aside. In the same pan, warm the oil, add in the onions, garlic and mushrooms, and cook for 4 minutes.
2. Stir in the beef, season with salt, black pepper and nutmeg, and sear until browned, about 2 minutes per side.
3. Preheat oven to 360 F and insert the pan in the oven to bake for 25 minutes. Remove the beef steaks to a bowl and cover with foil.
4. Place the pan over medium heat, pour in the heavy cream over the mushroom mixture, add in the reserved bacon and cook for 5 minutes; remove from heat. Spread the bacon/mushroom sauce over beef steaks, sprinkle with parsley and serve.

PER SERVING

Cal: 765 | Fat: 71g | Net Carbs: 3.8g | Protein 32g

Creamy Reuben Soup

Prep time: 20 minutes| Cook time: 19 minutes | | Serves 6

- 1 onion, diced
- 7 cups beef stock
- 1 tsp caraway seeds
- 2 garlic cloves, minced
- ¾ tsp black pepper
- 2 cups heavy cream
- 1 cup sauerkraut
- 1 pound corned beef, chopped
- 3 tbsp butter
- 1½ cups Swiss cheese
- Salt and black pepper to taste

1. Melt the butter in a large pot. Add onions and celery, and fry for 3 minutes until tender. Add garlic, and cook for another minute.
2. Pour the broth over and stir in sauerkraut, salt, caraway seeds, and add a pinch of pepper. Bring to a boil. Reduce the heat to low, and add the corned beef. Cook for about 15 minutes.
3. Adjust the seasoning. Stir in heavy cream and cheese, and cook for 1 minute.

PER SERVING

Cal: 450 | Net Carbs: 8g | Fat: 37g | Protein 23g

Roasted Pumpkin Filled with Beef & Mushrooms

Prep time: 1 hour 15 minutes | Cook time: 50 minutes | Serves 4

- 1½ lb pumpkin, pricked with a fork
- Salt and black pepper, to taste
- 1 garlic clove, minced
- 1 onion, chopped
- ½ cup mushrooms, sliced
- 28 ounces canned diced tomatoes
- ¼ tsp cayenne pepper
- ½ tsp dried thyme
- 1 pound ground beef
- 1 cup cauli rice

1. Preheat the oven to 430 F. Lay the pumpkin on a lined baking sheet and bake in the oven for 40 minutes. Cut in half, set aside to cool, deseed, scoop out most of the flesh and let sit.
2. Heat a greased pan over high heat, add in garlic, mushrooms, onion and beef, and cook until the meat browns.
3. Stir in green pepper, salt, thyme, tomatoes, black pepper, and cayenne, and cook for 10 minutes; stir in flesh and cauli rice. Stuff the squash halves with beef mixture, and bake in the oven for 10 minutes.

PER SERVING

Cal: 422 | Fat: 20g | Net Carbs: 9.8g | Protein 33.4g

Asian Spiced Beef with Broccoli

Prep time: 30 minutes | Cook time: 20 minutes | Serves 4

- ½ cup coconut milk
- 2 tbsp coconut oil
- ¼ tsp garlic powder
- ¼ tsp onion powder
- ½ tbsp coconut aminos
- 1 pound beef steak, cut into strips
- Salt and black pepper, to taste
- 1 head broccoli, cut into florets
- ½ tbsp thai green curry paste
- 1 tsp ginger paste
- 1 tbsp cilantro, chopped
- ½ tbsp sesame seeds

1. Warm coconut oil in a pan over medium heat, add in beef, season with garlic powder, pepper, salt, ginger paste, and onion powder and cook for 4 minutes. Mix in the broccoli and stir-fry for 5 minutes.
2. Pour in the coconut milk, coconut aminos, and thai curry paste and cook for 15 minutes.
3. Serve sprinkled with cilantro and sesame seeds.

PER SERVING

Cal: 623 | Fat: 43.2g | Net Carbs: 2.3g | Protein 53.5g

Red Wine Lamb with Mint & Sage

Prep time: 40 minutes | Cook time: 33 minutes | Serves 4

- 1 tbsp olive oil
- 1 pound lamb chops
- ½ tbsp sage
- ½ tsp mint
- ½ onion, sliced
- 1 garlic clove, minced
- ¼ cup red wine
- Salt and black pepper, to taste

1. Heat the olive oil in a pan. Add onion and garlic and cook for 3 minutes, until soft. Rub the sage and mint over the lamb chops. Cook the lamb for about 3 minutes per side; set aside.
2. Pour the red wine and 1 cup of water into the pan, bring the mixture to a boil. Cook until the liquid is reduced by half. Add the chops in the pan, reduce the heat, and let simmer for 30 minutes.

PER SERVING

Cal: 402 | Fat: 29.6g | Net Carbs: 3.8g | Protein 14.7g

Portobello Mushroom Beef Cheeseburgers

Prep time: 15 minutes | Cook time: 14 minutes | Serves 4

- 2 tbsp olive oil
- 1 lb ground beef
- ½ tsp fresh parsley, chopped
- ½ tsp Worcestershire sauce
- Salt and black pepper to taste
- 2 slices mozzarella cheese
- 2 portobello mushroom caps

1. In a bowl, mix the beef, parsley, Worcestershire sauce, salt and black pepper with your hands until evenly combined. Make medium-sized patties out of the mixture.
2. Preheat a grill to 400 F and coat the mushroom caps with olive oil, salt and black pepper.
3. Lay portobello caps, rounded side up and burger patties onto the hot grill pan and cook for 5 minutes. Turn the mushroom caps and continue cooking for 1 minute.
4. Lay a mozzarella slice on top of each patty. Continue cooking until the mushroom caps are softened, 4-5 minutes. Flip the patties and top with cheese. Cook for another 2-3 minutes until the cheese melts onto the meat. Remove the patties and sandwich into two mushroom caps each.

PER SERVING

Cal: 505 | Fat: 38.5g | Net Carbs: 3.2g | Protein 38g

Creamy Pork Chops with Thyme

Prep time: 25 minutes | Cook time: 11 minutes | Serves 6

- 7 strips bacon, chopped
- 6 pork chops
- Pink salt and black pepper to taste
- 5 sprigs fresh thyme
- ¼ cup chicken broth
- ½ cup heavy cream

1. Cook bacon in a large skillet over medium heat for 5 minutes to crispy. Remove with a slotted spoon onto a paper towel-lined plate to soak up excess fat. Season pork chops with salt and black pepper, and brown in the bacon grease for 4 minutes on each side. Remove to the bacon plate.
2. Stir the thyme, chicken broth, and heavy cream in the same skillet, and simmer for 5 minutes. Season with salt and black pepper. Put the chops and bacon in the skillet, and cook further for another 2 minutes. Serve chops and a generous ladle of sauce with cauli mash.

PER SERVING

Cal: 435 | Net Carbs: 3g | Fat: 37g | Protein 22g

Jerked Beef Stew

Prep time: 1 hour 10 minutes | Cook time: 1 hour 6 minutes | Serves 4

- 1 onion, chopped
- 2 tbsp olive oil
- 1 tsp ginger paste
- 1 tsp soy sauce
- 1 pound beef stew meat, cubed
- 1 red bell pepper, seeded and chopped
- ½ scotch bonnet pepper, chopped
- 2 green chilies, chopped
- 1 cup tomatoes, chopped
- 1 tbsp fresh cilantro, chopped
- 1 garlic clove, minced
- ¼ cup vegetable broth
- Salt and black pepper, to taste
- ¼ cup black olives, chopped
- 1 tsp jerk seasoning

1. Brown the beef on all sides in warm olive oil over medium heat; remove and set aside. Stir-fry in the red bell peppers, green chilies, jerk seasoning, garlic, scotch bonnet pepper, onion, ginger paste, and soy sauce, for about 5-6 minutes. Pour in the tomatoes and broth, and cook for 1 hour.
2. Stir in the olives, adjust the seasonings and serve sprinkled with fresh cilantro.

PER SERVING

Cal: 235 | Fat: 13.4g | Net Carbs: 2.8g | Protein 25.8g

Slow Cooker Carnitas

Prep time: 15 minutes | Cook time: 8 to 10 minutes | Serves 2

- Carnitas
- 2 medium onions, chopped, divided
- 1½ cups chicken broth Juice of 1 lime
- 1 (4 ½-pound) bone-in pork shoulder, or 1 (3-pound) boneless pork shoulder ½ cup chopped fresh cilantro
- Salt and pepper
- Dry Rub
- 1 tablespoon garlic powder
- 2 teaspoons chili powder
- 2 teaspoons ground cumin
- 2 teaspoons salt
- For Serving
- 1 to 2 heads butter lettuce, leaves separated
- 1 avocado, peeled, pitted, and sliced
- Chopped fresh cilantro
- Diced red onions
- 1 lime, cut into wedges

1. In a slow cooker, combine half of the chopped onions, the chicken broth, and the lime juice.
2. Rinse the pork shoulder with cold water and pat dry.
3. In a bowl, combine the dry rub ingredients. Rub the mixture over the entire pork shoulder.
4. Place the seasoned pork shoulder in the slow cooker on top of the onion mixture. Top with the remaining onions and the cilantro. Cover and cook on low for 8 to 10 hours, until the pork is fully cooked and shreds easily.
5. Remove the pork from the slow cooker, leaving the juices in the slow cooker. Shred the meat and return it to the pot with the juices; season to taste with salt and pepper, if needed. Cover and place on the keep warm setting for 30 minutes.
6. Preheat the oven to 400°F. Place the shredded pork on a rimmed baking sheet and bake for 15 to 20 minutes until crisp.
7. Serve in butter lettuce leaves topped with avocado slices, chopped cilantro, and diced red onions, with the lime wedges on the side.

PER SERVING

Calories: 376 | Fat: 24 g | Protein: 31.5 g | Total Carbs: 2.4 g | Net Carbs: 2 g

Cocktail Chili Beef Meatballs

Prep time: 45 minutes | Cook time: 20 minutes |Serves 4

- 2 tbsp olive oil
- 2 tbsp thyme
- ½ cup pork rinds, crushed
- 1 egg
- Salt and black pepper, to taste
- 1½ pounds ground beef
- 10 ounces canned onion soup
- 1 tbsp almond flour
- 2 tbsp chili sauce
- ¼ cup free-sugar ketchup
- 3 tsp Worcestershire sauce
- ½ tsp dry mustard

1. In a bowl, combine 1/3 cup of the onion soup with the beef, pepper, thyme, pork rinds, egg, and salt. Shape meatballs from the beef mixture. Heat olive oil in a pan over medium heat and place in the meatballs to brown on both sides.
2. In a bowl, combine the rest of the soup with the almond flour, dry mustard, ketchup, Worcestershire sauce, and ¼ cup of water. Pour this over the beef meatballs, cover the pan, and cook for 20 minutes.

PER SERVING

Cal: 341 | Fat: 21g | Net Carbs: 5.6g | Protein 23.5g

Veggie Beef Stew with Root Mash

Prep time: 1 hour 50 minutes | Cook time: 2 hours 5 minutes |Serves 4

- 1 tbsp olive oil
- 1 parsnip, chopped
- 1 garlic clove, minced
- 1 onion, chopped
- 1 celery stalk, chopped
- 1 pound stewing beef, cut into chunks
- Salt and black pepper to taste
- 1¼ cups beef stock
- 2 bay leaves
- 1 carrot, chopped
- ½ tbsp fresh rosemary, chopped
- 1 tomato, chopped
- 2 tbsp red wine
- ½ cauliflower head, cut into florets
- ½ celeriac, chopped
- 2 tbsp butter

1. In a pot, cook the celery, onion, and garlic, in warm oil over medium heat for 5 minutes. Stir in the beef chunks, and cook for 3 minutes. Season with salt and black pepper. Deglaze the bottom of the pot by adding the red wine. Add in the carrot, parsnip, beef stock, tomato, and bay leaves. Boil the mixture, reduce the heat to low and cook for 1 hour and 30 minutes.
2. Heat a pot with water over medium heat. Place in the celeriac, cover and simmer for 10 minutes. Add in the cauliflower florets, cook for 15 minutes, drain everything and combine with butter, pepper and salt. Mash using a potato masher and split the mash between 2 plates. Top with vegetable mixture and stewed beef, sprinkle with rosemary and serve.

PER SERVING

Cal: 465 | Fat: 24.5g | Net Carbs: 9.8g | Protein 32g

Creole Beef Tripe Stew

Prep time: 30 minutes | Cook time: 12 minutes | Serves 6

- 1 ½ lb beef tripe
- 4 cups buttermilk
- Pink salt to taste
- 2 tsp Creole seasoning
- 3 tbsp olive oil
- 3 tomatoes, diced

1. Put tripe in a bowl, and cover with buttermilk. Refrigerate for 3 hours to extract bitterness and gamey taste. Remove from buttermilk, pat dry with paper towels, and season with salt and creole seasoning.
2. Heat 2 tablespoons of oil in a skillet over medium heat and brown the tripe on both sides for 6 minutes in total. Remove, and set aside. Add the remaining oil, and sauté onions for 3 minutes. Include the tomatoes and cook for 10 minutes. Put the tripe in the sauce, and cook for 3 minutes.

PER SERVING

Cal: 342 | Net Carbs: 1g | Fat: 27g | Protein 22g

Sunny Side Up Burgers

Prep time: 10 minutes | Cook time:15 minutes |Serves 4

- 1 pound ground beef
- 2 teaspoons garlic powder
- Salt and pepper
- 4 slices cheddar cheese
- 1 tablespoon unsalted butter
- 4 large eggs
- 1 medium avocado, sliced
- 1 small tomato, cut into 4 slices
- ½ small yellow onion, sliced
- 4 butter lettuce leaves, for serving (optional)

1. Preheat a grill or grill pan to medium-high heat.
2. In a bowl, combine the ground beef and garlic powder. Season generously with salt and pepper and mix well. Use your hands to form the mixture into four ½-inch patties.
3. Grill the patties for 3 to 4 minutes on each side for medium-done burgers, flipping once. After flipping the patties, top each patty with a slice of cheese and allow to melt while the other side cooks.
4. In a skillet over medium heat, melt the butter. Crack the eggs into the pan and fry until cooked to your liking. (I recommend sunny side up or over easy.)
5. Place the burgers on a plate and top each burger with a slice of tomato, onion slices, avocado slices, and a fried egg. Season to taste with salt and pepper. Eat as is or enjoy wrapped in a butter lettuce leaf.

PER SERVING

Calories: 459 | Fat: 33.8 g | Protein: 34 g | Total Carbs: 5 g | Net Carbs: 2.3 g

Beef, Broccoli & Rosemary Slow Cooked Stew

Prep time: 4 hours 15 minutes | Cook time: 4 hours |Serves 4

- 2 tbsp olive oil
- 1 pound ground beef
- ½ cup leeks, chopped
- 1 head broccoli, cut into florets
- Salt and black pepper, to taste
- 1 tsp yellow mustard
- 1 tsp Worcestershire sauce
- 2 tomatoes, chopped
- 8 ounces tomato sauce
- 1 tbsp fresh rosemary, chopped
- ½ tsp dried oregano

1. Coat the broccoli with black pepper and salt. Set them into a bowl, drizzle over the olive oil, and toss to combine. In a separate bowl, combine the beef with Worcestershire sauce, leeks, salt, mustard, and black pepper, and stir well. Press on the slow cooker's bottom.
2. Scatter in the broccoli, add the tomatoes, oregano, and tomato sauce. Cook for 4 hours on high; covered. Serve the casserole with scattered rosemary.

PER SERVING

Cal: 677 | Fat: 42.1g | Net Carbs: 8.3g | Protein 63g

Pork Chops with Raspberry Sauce

Prep time: 18 minutes | Cook time: 9 minutes | Serves 4

- 2 tbsp olive oil
- 2 lb pork chops
- Salt and black pepper to taste
- 2 cups raspberries
- ¼ cup water
- 1 ½ tbsp Italian herb mix
- 3 tbsp balsamic vinegar
- 2 tsp Worcestershire sauce

1. Heat oil in a skillet over medium heat, season the pork with salt and black pepper and cook for 5 minutes on each side. Put in serving plates, and reserve the pork drippings.
2. Mash raspberries with a fork in a bowl until jam-like. Pour into a saucepan, add water, and herb mix. Cook on low heat for 4 minutes. Stir in pork drippings, vinegar, and Worcestershire sauce. Simmer for 1 minute. Dish the pork chops, spoon sauce over, and serve with braised rapini.

PER SERVING

Cal: 413 | Net Carbs: 1.1g | Fat: 32.5g | Protein 26.3g

Mini Beef & Mushroom Meatloaf

Prep time: 1 hour and 15 minutes | Cook time: 50 minutes | Serves 4

MEATLOAF:

- 1 pound ground beef
- ½ onion, chopped
- 1 tbsp almond milk
- 1 tbsp almond flour
- 1 small egg
- Salt and black pepper to taste
- 1 tbsp parsley, chopped
- 1/3 cup Parmesan cheese, grated

GLAZE:

- 1/3 cup balsamic vinegar
- ¼ tbsp xylitol
- ¼ tsp tomato paste
- ¼ tsp garlic powder
- ¼ tsp onion powder
- 1 tbsp ketchup, sugar-free

1. Grease a loaf pan with cooking spray and set aside. Preheat oven to 390 F. Combine all meatloaf ingredients in a large bowl. Press this mixture into the prepared loaf pan. Bake for about 30 minutes.
2. To make the glaze, whisk all ingredients in a bowl. Pour the glaze over the meatloaf. Put the meatloaf back in the oven and cook for 20 more minutes. Let meatloaf sit for 10 minutes before slicing.

PER SERVING

Cal: 311 | Fat: 21.3g | Net Carbs: 5.5g | Protein 24.2g

Casserole with Beef & Cauliflower

Prep time: 30 minutes | Cook time: 30 minutes | Serves 4

- 2 tbsp olive oil
- 1 pound ground beef
- Salt and black pepper to taste
- ½ cup cauli rice
- 1 tbsp parsley, chopped
- ½ tsp dried oregano
- 1 cup kohlrabi, chopped
- 5 oz can diced tomatoes
- ¼ cup water
- ½ cup mozzarella cheese, shredded

1. Put beef in a pot and season with salt and pepper; cook over medium heat for 6 minutes until no longer pink. Add cauli rice, kohlrabi, tomatoes, and water. Stir and bring to boil for 5 minutes to thicken the sauce. Spoon the beef mixture into the baking dish and spread evenly.
2. Sprinkle with cheese and bake in the oven for 15 minutes at 380 F until cheese has melted and it's golden brown. Remove and cool for 4 minutes, and serve sprinkled with parsley.

PER SERVING

Cal: 391 | Fat: 23.6g | Net Carbs: 7.3g | Protein 19.5g

Gyro Lettuce Wraps

Prep time: 10 minutes | Cook time: 20 to 25 minutes | Serves 2

MEATBALLS

- ½ pound ground beef
- ½ pound ground lamb
- 1 large egg
- ¼ cup finely chopped yellow onions
- 1 tablespoon minced garlic
- 1 teaspoon ground cumin
- ½ teaspoon dried ground oregano
- ½ teaspoon salt
- ½ teaspoon ground black pepper
- ⅓ cup crumbled feta cheese

FOR SERVING

- 8 butter lettuce leaves or other lettuce wraps of choice 1 large tomato, sliced
- ¼ red onion, thinly sliced
- ½ batch Tzatziki Sauce

1. Preheat the oven to 400°F and line a rimmed baking sheet with parchment paper.
2. In a large bowl, combine all the meatball ingredients except for the feta cheese and use your hands to incorporate. Carefully fold in the feta.
3. Form the mixture into sixteen 1-inch meatballs and place on the lined baking sheet, spaced at least 1 inch apart.
4. Bake the meatballs for 20 to 25 minutes, until the outsides are browned and the internal temperature reaches 160°F.
5. Let cool for 5 minutes, then cut each meatball into 3 slices.
6. To assemble the wraps, divide the meatball slices evenly among the lettuce leaves. Top with tomato and red onion slices and tzatziki sauce.

PER SERVING

Calories: 396 | Fat: 27.3 g | Protein: 29 g | Total Carbs: 8.1 g | Net Carbs: 6 g

Bunless Philly Cheesesteaks

Prep time: 15 minutes | Cook time:10 minutes |Serves 2

- 1 tablespoon unsalted butter
- 1 cup white mushrooms, halved
- ½ cup chopped onions
- ⅓ cup chopped green bell peppers
- ¼ teaspoon garlic powder
- 8 ounces rare roast beef slices
- 2 slices provolone cheese
- Salt and pepper

1. In a medium-sized saucepan over medium heat, melt the butter. Add the mushrooms, onions, bell peppers, and garlic powder and cook until the veggies are soft, 4 to 5 minutes.
2. Cut the roast beef into 1-inch squares.
3. Add the roast beef to the saucepan and toss with the vegetables for 1
4. minute, until heated through.
5. Reduce the heat to low and top the roast beef and veggie mixture with the provolone cheese. Cover the pan with a lid for 2 to 3 minutes to allow the cheese to melt. Season with salt and pepper to taste, then serve.

PER SERVING

Calories: 305 | Fat: 16 g | Protein: 33 g | Total Carbs: 6 g | Net Carbs: 4.5 g

Cilantro Beef Curry with Cauliflower

Prep time: 26 minutes | Cook time: 21 minutes |Serves 4

- 1 tbsp olive oil
- ½ lb ground beef
- 1 garlic clove, minced
- 1 tsp turmeric
- 1 tbsp cilantro, chopped
- 1 tbsp ginger paste
- ½ tsp garam masala
- 5 oz canned whole tomatoes
- 1 head cauliflower, cut into florets
- Salt and chili pepper to taste
- ¼ cup water

1. Heat oil in a saucepan over medium heat, add the beef, garlic, ginger paste, and garam masala. Cook for 5 minutes while breaking any lumps.
2. Stir in the tomatoes and cauliflower, season with salt, turmeric, and chili pepper, and cook covered for 6 minutes. Add the water and bring to a boil over medium heat for 10 minutes or until the water has reduced by half. Spoon the curry into serving bowls and serve sprinkled with cilantro.

PER SERVING

Cal: 365 | Fat: 31.6g | Net Carbs: 3.5g | Protein 19.5g

Pan-Seared Steak with Mushroom Sauce

Prep time: 5 minutes | Cook time: 15 minutes | Serves 4

- 4 top sirloin steaks (6 ounces each), at room temperature
- ½ teaspoon sea salt, or more to taste
- ¼ teaspoon black pepper, or more to taste
- 4 tablespoons (½ stick) butter, divided into 2 tablespoons and 2 tablespoons
- 2 cloves garlic, minced
- 8 ounces (~3 cups) baby portobello mushrooms, thinly sliced
- ¼ cup beef broth
- 1 teaspoon fresh thyme, chopped
- ¼ cup heavy cream

1. Season the steaks on both sides with the sea salt and black pepper. Let rest at room temperature for 30 minutes.
2. Heat a large sauté pan over medium-high heat. Add 2 tablespoons of the butter and melt.
3. Place the steaks in the pan in a single layer. Cook for the following number of minutes on each side, based on desired level of doneness (cook time will vary depending on the steak's thickness and the temperature of the pan). For best results, use a meat thermometer and remove the steak from the heat when it's 5°F lower than the desired final temperature. Steaks will rise another 5°F while resting.
4. When the steaks in the pan reach the desired internal temperature, remove them from the pan, transfer to a plate, and cover with foil. Let the steaks rest without cutting: the steak's internal temperature will rise another 5°F to the desired final temperature.
5. Return the sauté pan to medium heat. Melt the remaining 2 tablespoons butter. Add the garlic and sauté for about 1 minute, until fragrant.
6. Add the mushrooms, beef broth, and thyme. Scrape any browned bits from the bottom of the pan. Adjust the heat to bring to a simmer (typically at medium-high), cover, and simmer, stirring occasionally, for 5 to 8 minutes, until the mushrooms are soft.
7. Reduce the heat to medium, add the cream, and simmer for 1 to 3 minutes, until the sauce thickens. Adjust salt and pepper to taste, if needed.
8. Spoon the mushroom sauce over the steaks to serve.

PER SERVING

Calories: 420 | Fat: 27g | Total Carbs: 3g | Net Carbs: 3g | Protein: 39g

Kung Pao Beef

Prep time: 5 minutes | Cook time: 15 minutes | Serves 4

SAUCE/MARINADE:

- ¼ cup coconut aminos
- 1½ tablespoons white wine vinegar
- 1½ tablespoons sherry wine
- 1 tablespoon avocado oil
- 1 teaspoon chili paste

STIR-FRY:

- 1 pound flank steak, thinly sliced against the grain and cut into bite-size pieces
- 2 tablespoons avocado oil, divided into 1 tablespoon and 1 tablespoon
- 2 medium bell peppers (6 ounces each), red and green, chopped into bite-size pieces
- 2 cloves garlic, minced
- ¼ cup roasted peanuts

MAKE THE SAUCE/MARINADE:

1. In a small bowl, whisk together the coconut aminos, white wine vinegar, sherry wine, avocado oil, and chili paste.

MAKE THE STIR-FRY:

1. Place the sliced steak into a medium bowl. Pour half of the sauce/marinade (about ¼ cup) over it and stir to coat. Cover and chill for at least 30 minutes, up to 2 hours.
2. About 10 minutes before marinating time is up or when you are ready to cook, in a large wok or sauté pan, heat 1 tablespoon of the oil over medium-high heat. Add the bell peppers and sauté for 7 to 8 minutes, until soft and browned.
3. Add the garlic and sauté for about 1 minute, until fragrant.
4. Remove the peppers and garlic, and cover to keep warm.
5. Add the remaining 1 tablespoon oil to the pan and heat over very high heat. Add the steak, arrange in a single layer, and cook undisturbed for 2 to 4 minutes per side, until browned on each side. If it's not cooked through yet, you can stir-fry for longer. Remove the meat from the pan and cover to keep warm.
6. Add the reserved marinade to the pan. Bring to a vigorous simmer and continue to simmer for a few minutes, until thickened.
7. Add the cooked meat, cooked peppers, and roasted peanuts to the pan and toss in the sauce.

PER SERVING

Calories: 341 | Fat: 20g | Total Carbs: 9g | Net Carbs: 7g | Protein: 27g

Flank Steak Roll

Prep time: 42 minutes | Cook time: 30 minutes | Serves 4

- 1 lb flank steak
- Salt and black pepper to taste
- ½ cup ricotta cheese, crumbled
- ½ cup baby kale, chopped
- 1 serrano pepper, chopped
- 1 tbsp basil leaves, chopped

1. Wrap the steak in plastic wraps, place on a flat surface, and gently run a rolling pin over to flatten. Take off the wraps. Sprinkle with half of the ricotta cheese, top with kale, serrano pepper, and the remaining cheese. Roll the steak over on the stuffing and secure with toothpicks.
2. Place in the greased baking sheet and cook for 30 minutes at 390 F, flipping once until nicely browned on the outside and the cheese melted within. Cool for 3 minutes, slice and serve with basil.

PER SERVING

Cal: 445 | Fat: 21g | Net Carbs: 2.8g | Protein 53g

Chapter 7
Fish & Seafood

Salmon Crusted with Pistachio Nuts and Sauce

Prep time: 35 minutes | Cook time: 20 minutes | Serves 4

- 4 salmon fillets
- ½ tsp pepper
- 1 tsp salt
- ¼ cup mayonnaise
- ½ cup pistachios, chopped
- Sauce
- 1 shallot, chopped
- 2 tsp lemon zest
- 1 tbsp olive oil
- A pinch of pepper
- 1 cup heavy cream

1. Preheat the oven to 375 F. Brush the salmon with mayonnaise and season with salt and pepper. Coat with pistachios. Place in a lined baking dish, and bake, for 15 minutes.
2. Heat the olive oil in a saucepan, and sauté the shallots, for a few minutes. Stir in the rest of the sauce ingredients. Bring to a boil, and cook until thickened. Serve the salmon topped with the sauce.

PER SERVING

Cal: 563 | Net Carbs: 6g | Fat: 47g | Protein 34g

Greek Tilapia with Herbs

Prep time: 30 minutes | Cook time: 16 minutes | Serves 4

- 4 tilapia fillets
- 2 garlic cloves, minced
- 2 tsp oregano
- 14 ounces tomatoes, diced
- 1 tbsp olive oil
- ½ red onion, chopped
- 2 tbsp parsley
- ¼ cup kalamata olives

1. Heat olive oil in a skillet over medium heat, and cook onion, garlic, and oregano for 3 minutes. Stir in tomatoes and bring the mixture to a boil. Reduce the heat and simmer, for 5 minutes.
2. Add olives and tilapia. Cook, for about 8 minutes. Serve the tilapia with the tomato sauce.

PER SERVING

Cal: 182 | Net Carbs: 6g | Fat: 15g | Protein 23g

Easy Shrimp with Red Wine Sauce

Prep time: 45 minutes| Cook time: 30 minutes | Serves 4

- 1 pound shrimp, peeled and deveined
- 2 tbsp olive oil
- Juice of 1 lime
- Red wine sauce:
- ½ tsp salt
- ¼ cup olive oil
- 2 garlic cloves
- ¼ cup red onion, chopped
- ¼ cup red wine vinegar
- ½ tsp pepper
- 2 cups parsley
- ¼ tsp red pepper flakes

1. Place the sauce ingredients in the blender. Process until smooth. Set aside. Combine shrimp, olive oil and lime juice in a bowl, and let marinate in the fridge, for 30 minutes.
2. Preheat your grill to medium. Add shrimp, and cook about 2 minutes per side. Serve shrimp drizzled with the sauce.

PER SERVING

Cal: 283 | Net Carbs: 3.5g | Fat: 20.3g | Protein 16g

Crispy Salmon with Broccoli & Red Bell Pepper

Prep time: 30 minutes | Cook time: 22 minutes |Serves 4

- 4 salmon fillets
- Salt and black pepper to taste
- 2 tbsp mayonnaise
- 2 tbsp fennel seeds, crushed
- ½ head broccoli, cut in florets
- 1 red bell pepper, sliced
- 1 tbsp olive oil
- 2 lemon wedges

1. Brush the salmon with mayonnaise and season with salt and black pepper. Coat with fennel seeds, place in a lined baking dish and bake for 15 minutes at 370 F. Steam the broccoli and carrot for 3-4 minutes, or until tender, in a pot over medium heat.
2. Heat the olive oil in a saucepan and sauté the red bell pepper for 5 minutes. Stir in the broccoli and turn off the heat. Let the pan sit on the warm burner for 2-3 minutes. Serve with baked salmon garnished with lemon wedges.

PER SERVING

Cal: 563 | Fat: 37g | Net Carbs: 6g | Protein 54g

Saucy Mustard Salmon

Prep time: 15 minutes | Cook time: 6 minutes | Serves 4

- 4 salmon fillets
- ¾ tsp fresh thyme
- 1 tbsp butter
- ¾ tsp tarragon
- Salt and black pepper to taste
- Sauce
- ¼ cup Dijon mustard
- 2 tbsp white wine
- ½ tsp tarragon
- ¼ cup heavy cream

1. Season the salmon with thyme, tarragon, salt, and black pepper. Melt the butter in a pan over medium heat. Add salmon and cook for about 4-5 minutes on both sides until the salmon is cooked through. Remove to a warm dish and cover.
2. To the same pan, add the sauce ingredients over low heat and simmer until the sauce is slightly thickened, stirring continually. Cook for 60 seconds to infuse the flavors and adjust the seasoning. Serve the salmon, topped with the sauce.

PER SERVING

Cal: 537 | Fat: 26.4g | Net Carbs: 1.5g | Protein 67g

Simple Lemon Herb Whitefish

Prep time: 5 minutes | Cook time: 15 minutes | Serves 6

- 6 white fish fillets (~5 ounces each), preferably lake whitefish, grouper, or halibut
- 1 teaspoon sea salt
- ½ teaspoon black pepper
- 3 tablespoons olive oil
- 2 teaspoons lemon zest
- 2 teaspoons lemon juice
- 2 cloves garlic, minced
- 1 teaspoon minced capers (optional)
- 3 tablespoons minced fresh parsley
- 3 tablespoons minced fresh dill

1. Preheat the oven to 400°F. Line a sheet pan with foil or parchment paper and grease lightly.
2. Place the fish fillets in a single layer on the pan. Season the fish on both sides with the sea salt and black pepper.
3. In a small bowl, whisk together the oil, lemon zest, lemon juice, garlic, capers (if using), parsley, and dill. Spoon about 1 tablespoon of the lemon-herb oil over each piece of fish, then use a brush to spread it.
4. Bake for 10 to 14 minutes, depending on the thickness of the fish, until the fish flakes easily with a fork.

PER SERVING

Calories: 325 | Fat: 17g | Total Carbs: 0g | Net Carbs: 0g | Protein: 37g

Zucchini Noodles with Sardines & Capers

Prep time: 10 minutes | Cook time: 11 minutes | Serves 2

- 4 cups zoodles
- 2 ounces cubed bacon
- 4 ounces canned sardines, chopped
- ½ cup canned tomatoes, chopped
- 1 tbsp capers
- 1 tbsp parsley
- 1 tsp garlic, minced

1. Pour some of the sardine oil in a pan. Cook garlic and bacon for 3 minutes. Stir in the tomatoes, and let simmer, for 5 minutes.
2. Add zoodles and sardines, and cook, for 3 minutes.

PER SERVING

Cal: 230 | Net Carbs: 6g | Fat: 31g | Protein 20g

Maple Pecan-Crusted Salmon

Prep time: 5 minutes | Cook time: 15 minutes | Serves 4

- 4 salmon fillets (4 ounces each)
- 4 tablespoons (½ stick) butter, melted
- 2 tablespoons powdered erythritol
- ½ teaspoon real maple extract
- ½ teaspoon smoked paprika
- ½ teaspoon sea salt
- ¼ teaspoon cayenne pepper, or less if you prefer a milder marinade
- ¾ cup pecans

1. Preheat the oven to 400°F. Line a large baking sheet with foil.
2. Arrange the salmon fillets on the lined baking sheet.
3. In a medium bowl, make the maple glaze. Whisk together the melted butter, powdered erythritol, maple extract, smoked paprika, sea salt, and cayenne pepper.
4. Brush both sides of the salmon with the maple glaze, using about half of it. Set the remaining glaze aside.
5. Pulse the pecans in a food processor until finely chopped. Don't overmix or it will turn into pecan flour. (Alternatively, chop with a knife.) Add the chopped pecans to the remaining glaze and stir together to coat.
6. Spoon the pecan mixture evenly over the salmon fillets, pressing on the top with your hands.
7. Bake for 9 to 12 minutes, until the fish flakes easily with a fork.

PER SERVING

Calories: 392 | Fat: 32g | Total Carbs: 7g | Net Carbs: 1g | Protein: 24g

Chili Cod with Chive Sauce

Prep time: 20 minutes | Cook time: 18 minutes |Serves 4

- 1 tsp chili powder
- 4 cod fillets
- Salt and black pepper to taste
- 1 tbsp olive oil
- 1 garlic clove, minced
- 1/3 cup lemon juice
- 2 tbsp vegetable stock
- 2 tbsp chives, chopped

1. Preheat oven to 400 F and grease a baking dish with cooking spray. Rub the cod fillets with chili powder, salt, and pepper and lay in the dish. Bake for 10-15 minutes.
2. In a skillet over low heat, warm olive oil and sauté garlic for 1 minute. Add lemon juice, vegetable stock, and chives. Season with salt, pepper, and cook for 3 minutes until the stock slightly reduces. Divide fish into 2 plates, top with sauce, and serve.

PER SERVING

Cal: 448 | Fat: 35.3g | Net Carbs: 6.3g | Protein 20g

Baked Haddock with Cheesy Hazelnut Topping

Prep time: 50 minutes | Cook time: 23 minutes |Serves 4

- 1 tbsp butter
- 1 shallot, sliced
- 1 pound haddock fillet
- 2 eggs, hard-boiled, chopped
- ½ cup water
- 3 tbsp hazelnut flour
- 2 cups sour cream
- 1 tbsp parsley, chopped
- ½ cup pork rinds, crushed
- 1 cup mozzarella cheese, grated
- Salt and black pepper to taste

1. Melt butter in a saucepan over medium heat and sauté the shallots for about 3 minutes.
2. Reduce the heat to low and stir the hazelnut flour into it to form a roux. Cook the roux to be golden brown and stir in the sour cream until the mixture is smooth. Season with salt and pepper, and stir in the parsley.
3. Spread the haddock fillet in a greased baking dish, sprinkle the eggs on top, and spoon the sauce over. In a bowl, mix the pork rinds with the mozzarella cheese, and sprinkle it over the sauce.
4. Bake in the oven for 20 minutes at 370 F until the top is golden and the sauce and cheese are bubbly.

PER SERVING

Cal: 788 | Fat: 57g | Net Carbs: 8.5g | Protein 65g

Tuna Slow-Cooked In Olive Oil

Prep time: 5 minutes | Cook time: 45 minutes | Serves 4

- 1 cup extra-virgin olive oil, plus more if needed
- 4 (3- to 4-inch) sprigs fresh rosemary
- 8 (3- to 4-inch) sprigs fresh thyme
- 2 large garlic cloves, thinly sliced
- 2 (2-inch) strips lemon zest
- 1 teaspoon salt
- ½ teaspoon freshly ground black pepper
- 1 pound fresh tuna steaks (about 1 inch thick)

1. Select a thick pot just large enough to fit the tuna in a single layer on the bottom. The larger the pot, the more olive oil you will need to use. Combine the olive oil, rosemary, thyme, garlic, lemon zest, salt, and pepper over medium-low heat and cook until warm and fragrant, 20 to 25 minutes, lowering the heat if it begins to smoke.
2. Remove from the heat and allow to cool for 25 to 30 minutes, until warm but not hot.
3. Add the tuna to the bottom of the pan, adding additional oil if needed so that tuna is fully submerged, and return to medium-low heat. Cook for 5 to 10 minutes, or until the oil heats back up and is warm and fragrant but not smoking. Lower the heat if it gets too hot.
4. Remove the pot from the heat and let the tuna cook in warm oil 4 to 5 minutes, to your desired level of doneness. For a tuna that is rare in the center, cook for 2 to 3 minutes.
5. Remove from the oil and serve warm, drizzling 2 to 3 tablespoons seasoned oil over the tuna.
6. To store for later use, remove the tuna from the oil and place in a container with a lid. Allow tuna and oil to cool separately. When both have cooled, remove the herb stems with a slotted spoon and pour the cooking oil over the tuna. Cover and store in the refrigerator for up to 1 week. Bring to room temperature to allow the oil to liquify before serving.

PER SERVING

Calories: 363 | Total Fat: 28g | Total Carbs: 1g | Net Carbs: 1g | Fiber: 0g | Protein: 27g | Sodium: 624mg

Nut Crusted Baked Fish

Prep time: 10 minutes | Cook time: 20 minutes | Serves 4

- ½ cup extra-virgin olive oil, divided
- 1 pound flaky white fish (such as cod, haddock, or halibut), skin removed
- ½ cup shelled finely chopped pistachios
- ½ cup ground flaxseed
- Zest and juice of 1 lemon, divided
- 1 teaspoon ground cumin
- 1 teaspoon ground allspice
- ½ teaspoon salt (use 1 teaspoon if pistachios are unsalted)
- ¼ teaspoon freshly ground black pepper

1. Preheat the oven to 400°F.
2. Line a baking sheet with parchment paper or aluminum foil and drizzle 2 tablespoons olive oil over the sheet, spreading to evenly coat the bottom.
3. Cut the fish into 4 equal pieces and place on the prepared baking sheet.
4. In a small bowl, combine the pistachios, flaxseed, lemon zest, cumin, allspice, salt, and pepper. Drizzle in ¼ cup olive oil and stir well.
5. Divide the nut mixture evenly atop the fish pieces. Drizzle the lemon juice and remaining 2 tablespoons oil over the fish and bake until cooked through, 15 to 20 minutes, depending on the thickness of the fish.

PER SERVING

Calories: 509 | Total Fat: 41g | Total Carbs: 9g | Net Carbs: 3g | Fiber: 6g | Protein: 26g | Sodium: 331mg

Tilapia Cabbage Tortillas with Cauliflower Rice

Prep time: 20 minutes | Cook time: 12 minutes | Serves 4

- 1 tsp avocado oil
- 1 cup cauli rice
- 4 tilapia fillets, cut into cubes
- ¼ tsp taco seasoning
- Sea salt and hot paprika to taste
- 2 whole cabbage leaves
- 2 tbsp guacamole
- 1 tbsp cilantro, chopped

1. Microwave the cauli rice in microwave safe bowl for 4 minutes. Fluff with a fork and set aside.
2. Warm avocado oil in a skillet over medium heat, rub the tilapia with the taco seasoning, salt, and hot paprika, and fry until brown on all sides, for about 8 minutes in total. Divide the fish among the cabbage leaves, top with cauli rice, guacamole and cilantro.

PER SERVING

Cal: 170 | Fat: 6.4g | Net Carbs: 1.4g | Protein 24.5g

Shrimp Ceviche Salad

Prep time: 15 minutes | Cook time: 5 minutes | Serves 4

- 1 pound fresh shrimp, peeled and deveined
- 1 small red or yellow bell pepper, cut into ½-inch chunks
- ½ English cucumber, peeled and cut into ½-inch chunks
- ½ small red onion, cut into thin slivers
- ¼ cup chopped fresh cilantro or flat-leaf Italian parsley
- ⅓ cup freshly squeezed lime juice
- 2 tablespoons freshly squeezed lemon juice
- 2 tablespoons freshly squeezed clementine juice or orange juice
- ½ cup extra-virgin olive oil
- 1 teaspoon salt
- ½ teaspoon freshly ground black pepper
- 2 ripe avocados, peeled, pitted, and cut into ½-inch chunks

1. Cut the shrimp in half lengthwise. In a large glass bowl, combine the shrimp, bell pepper, cucumber, onion, and cilantro.
2. In a small bowl, whisk together the lime, lemon, and clementine juices, olive oil, salt, and pepper. Pour the mixture over the shrimp and veggies and toss to coat. Cover and refrigerate for at least 2 hours, or up to 8 hours. Give the mixture a toss every 30 minutes for the first 2 hours to make sure all the shrimp "cook" in the juices.
3. Add the cut avocado just before serving and toss to combine.

PER SERVING

Calories: 497 | Total Fat: 40g | Total Carbs: 14g | Net Carbs: 8g | Fiber: 6g | Protein: 25g | Sodium: 756mg

Speedy Salmon in Creamy Parsley Sauce

Prep time: 25 minutes | Cook time: 15 minutes | Serves 4

- 4 salmon fillets
- ½ cup heavy cream
- 1 tbsp mayonnaise
- ½ tbsp parsley, chopped
- ½ lemon, zested and juiced
- Salt and black pepper to season
- 1 tbsp Parmesan cheese, grated

1. In a bowl, mix the heavy cream, parsley, mayonnaise, lemon zest, lemon juice, salt and pepper, and set aside.
2. Season the fish with salt and black pepper, drizzle lemon juice on both sides of the fish and arrange them in a parchment paper-lined baking sheet.
3. Spread the parsley mixture and sprinkle with Parmesan cheese. Bake in the oven for 15 minutes at 400 F. Great served with steamed broccoli.

PER SERVING

Cal: 554 | Fat: 30.4g | Net Carbs: 2.2g | Protein 56.2g

Greek Stuffed Squid

Prep time: 15 minutes | Cook time: 30 minutes | Serves 4

- 8 ounces frozen spinach, thawed and drained (about 1½ cup)
- 4 ounces crumbled goat cheese
- ½ cup chopped pitted olives (I like Kalamata in this recipe)
- ½ cup extra-virgin olive oil, divided
- ¼ cup chopped sun-dried tomatoes
- ¼ cup chopped fresh flat-leaf Italian parsley
- 2 garlic cloves, finely minced
- ¼ teaspoon freshly ground black pepper
- 2 pounds baby squid, cleaned and tentacles removed

1. Preheat the oven to 350°F.
2. In a medium bowl, combine the spinach, goat cheese, olives, ¼ cup olive oil, sun-dried tomatoes, parsley, garlic, and pepper.
3. Pour 2 tablespoons olive oil in the bottom of an 8-inch square baking dish and spread to coat the bottom.
4. Stuff each cleaned squid with 2 to 3 tablespoons of the cheese mixture, depending on the size of squid, and place in the prepared baking dish.
5. Drizzle the tops with the remaining 2 tablespoons olive oil and bake until the squid are cooked through, 25 to 30 minutes. Remove from the oven and allow to cool 5 to 10 minutes before serving.

PER SERVING

Calories: 469 | Total Fat: 37g | Total Carbs: 10g | Net Carbs: 7g | Fiber: 3g | Protein: 24g | Sodium: 576mg

Seafood Fideo

Prep time: 15 minutes | Cook time: 20 minutes | Serves 6 to 8

- 2 tablespoons extra-virgin olive oil, plus ½ cup, divided
- 6 cups Zucchini Noodles, roughly chopped (2 to 3 medium zucchini)
- 1 pound shrimp, peeled, deveined and roughly chopped
- 6 to 8 ounces canned chopped clams, drained (about 3 to 4 ounces drained)
- 4 ounces crabmeat
- ½ cup crumbled goat cheese
- ½ cup crumbled feta cheese
- 1 (28-ounce) can chopped tomatoes, with their juices
- 1 teaspoon salt
- 1 teaspoon garlic powder
- ½ teaspoon smoked paprika
- ½ cup shredded Parmesan cheese
- ¼ cup chopped fresh flat-leaf Italian parsley, for garnish

1. Preheat the oven to 375°F.
2. Pour 2 tablespoons olive oil in the bottom of a 9-by-13-inch baking dish and swirl to coat the bottom.
3. In a large bowl, combine the zucchini noodles, shrimp, clams, and crabmeat.
4. In another bowl, combine the goat cheese, feta,

and ¼ cup olive oil and stir to combine well. Add the canned tomatoes and their juices, salt, garlic powder, and paprika and combine well. Add the mixture to the zucchini and seafood mixture and stir to combine.

5. Pour the mixture into the prepared baking dish, spreading evenly. Spread shredded Parmesan over top and drizzle with the remaining ¼ cup olive oil. Bake until bubbly, 20 to 25 minutes. Serve warm, garnished with chopped parsley.

PER SERVING

Calories: 434 | Total Fat: 31g | Total Carbs: 12g | Net Carbs: 9g | Fiber: 3g | Protein: 29g | Sodium: 712mg

Cod with Parsley Pistou

Prep time: 15 minutes | Cook time: 10 minutes | Serves 4

- 1 cup packed roughly chopped fresh flat-leaf Italian parsley
- 1 to 2 small garlic cloves, minced
- Zest and juice of 1 lemon
- 1 teaspoon salt
- ½ teaspoon freshly ground black pepper
- 1 cup extra-virgin olive oil, divided
- 1 pound cod fillets, cut into 4 equal-sized pieces

1. In a food processer, combine the parsley, garlic, lemon zest and juice, salt, and pepper. Pulse to chop well.
2. While the food processor is running, slowly stream in ¾ cup olive oil until well combined. Set aside.
3. In a large skillet, heat the remaining ¼ cup olive oil over medium-high heat. Add the cod fillets, cover, and cook 4 to 5 minutes on each side, or until cooked through. Thicker fillets may require a bit more cooking time. Remove from the heat and keep warm.
4. Add the pistou to the skillet and heat over medium-low heat. Return the cooked fish to the skillet, flipping to coat in the sauce. Serve warm, covered with pistou.

PER SERVING

Calories: 581 | Total Fat: 55g | Total Carbs: 3g | Net Carbs: 2g | Fiber: 1g | Protein: 21g | Sodium: 652mg

Salmon with Tarragon Dijon Sauce

Prep time: 5 minutes | Cook time: 15 minutes | Serves 4

- 1¼ pounds salmon fillet (skin on or removed), cut into 4 equal pieces
- ¼ cup avocado oil mayonnaise
- ¼ cup Dijon or stone-ground mustard
- Zest and juice of ½ lemon
- 2 tablespoons chopped fresh tarragon or 1 to 2 teaspoons dried tarragon
- ½ teaspoon salt
- ¼ teaspoon freshly ground black pepper
- 4 tablespoons extra-virgin olive oil, for serving

1. Preheat the oven to 425°F. Line a baking sheet with parchment paper.
2. Place the salmon pieces, skin-side down, on a baking sheet.
3. In a small bowl, whisk together the mayonnaise, mustard, lemon zest and juice, tarragon, salt, and pepper. Top the salmon evenly with the sauce mixture.
4. Bake until slightly browned on top and slightly translucent in the center, 10 to 12 minutes, depending on the thickness of the salmon. Remove from the oven and leave on the baking sheet for 10 minutes. Drizzle each fillet with 1 tablespoon olive oil before serving.

PER SERVING

Calories: 387 | Total Fat: 28g | Total Carbs: 4g | Net Carbs: 3g | Fiber: 1g | Protein: 29g | Sodium: 633mg

Smoked Salmon Crudités

Prep time: 10 minutes | Cook time: 5 minutes | Serves 4

- 6 ounces smoked wild salmon
- 2 tablespoons Roasted Garlic Aioli or avocado mayonnaise
- 1 tablespoon Dijon mustard
- 1 tablespoon chopped scallions, green parts only
- 2 teaspoons chopped capers
- ½ teaspoon dried dill
- 4 endive spears or hearts of romaine
- ½ English cucumber, cut into ¼-inch-thick rounds

1. Roughly chop the smoked salmon and place in a small bowl. Add the aioli, Dijon, scallions, capers, and dill and mix well.
2. Top endive spears and cucumber rounds with a spoonful of smoked salmon mixture and enjoy chilled.

PER SERVING

Calories: 92 | Total Fat: 5g | Total Carbs: 5g | Net Carbs: 4g | Fiber: 1g | Protein: 9g | Sodium: 472mg

Rosemary-Lemon Snapper Baked In Parchment

Prep time: 15 minutes | Cook time: 15 minutes | Serves 4

- 1¼ pounds fresh red snapper fillet, cut into two equal pieces
- 2 lemons, thinly sliced
- 6 to 8 sprigs fresh rosemary, stems removed or 1 to 2 tablespoons dried rosemary
- ½ cup extra-virgin olive oil
- 6 garlic cloves, thinly sliced
- 1 teaspoon salt
- ½ teaspoon freshly ground black pepper

1. Preheat the oven to 425°F.
2. Place two large sheets of parchment (about twice the size of each piece of fish) on the counter. Place 1 piece of fish in the center of each sheet.
3. Top the fish pieces with lemon slices and rosemary leaves.
4. In a small bowl, combine the olive oil, garlic, salt, and pepper. Drizzle the oil over each piece of fish.
5. Top each piece of fish with a second large sheet of parchment and starting on a long side, fold the paper up to about 1 inch from the fish. Repeat on the remaining sides, going in a clockwise direction. Fold in each corner once to secure.
6. Place both parchment pouches on a baking sheet and bake until the fish is cooked through, 10 to 12 minutes.

PER SERVING

Calories: 390 | Total Fat: 29g | Total Carbs: 3g | Net Carbs: 3g | Fiber: 0g | Protein: 29g | Sodium: 674mg

Round Zucchini Stuffed with Shrimp and Tomato

Prep time: 35 minutes | Cook time:28 minutes |Serves 2

- 1 lb zucchinis, tops removed and reserved
- 1 lb small shrimp, peeled, deveined
- ¼ onion, chopped
- 1 tsp olive oil
- 1 small tomato, chopped
- Salt and black pepper to taste
- 1 tbsp basil leaves, chopped

1. Scoop out the seeds of the zucchinis with a spoon and set aside.
2. Warm olive oil in a skillet and sauté the onion and tomato for 3 minutes. Add the shrimp, zucchini flesh, basil leaves, salt, and pepper and cook for another 5 minutes.
3. Fill the zucchini shells with the mixture. Cover with the zucchini tops and place them on a greased baking sheet to cook for 15 to 20 minutes at 390 F. The shrimp should no longer be pink by this time. Remove the zucchinis and serve with tomato and mozzarella salad.

PER SERVING

Cal: 252 | Fat: 6.4g | Net Carbs: 8.9g | Protein 37.6g

Tuna Croquettes

Prep time: 40 minutes | Cook time: 25 minutes | Serves 4

- 6 tablespoons extra-virgin olive oil, plus 1 to 2 cups
- 5 tablespoons almond flour, plus 1 cup, divided
- 1¼ cups heavy cream
- 1 (4-ounce) can olive oil-packed yellowfin tuna
- 1 tablespoon chopped red onion
- 2 teaspoons minced capers
- ½ teaspoon dried dill
- ¼ teaspoon freshly ground black pepper
- 2 large eggs
- 1 cup panko breadcrumbs (or a gluten-free version)

1. In a large skillet, heat 6 tablespoons olive oil over medium-low heat. Add 5 tablespoons almond flour and cook, stirring constantly, until a smooth paste forms and the flour browns slightly, 2 to 3 minutes.
2. Increase the heat to medium-high and gradually add the heavy cream, whisking constantly until completely smooth and thickened, another 4 to 5 minutes.
3. Remove from the heat and stir in the tuna, red onion, capers, dill, and pepper.
4. Transfer the mixture to an 8-inch square baking dish that is well coated with olive oil and allow to cool to room temperature. Cover and refrigerate until chilled, at least 4 hours or up to overnight.
5. To form the croquettes, set out three bowls. In one, beat together the eggs. In another, add the remaining almond flour. In the third, add the panko. Line a baking sheet with parchment paper.
6. Using a spoon, place about a tablespoon of cold prepared dough into the flour mixture and roll to coat. Shake off excess and, using your hands, roll into an oval.
7. Dip the croquette into the beaten egg, then lightly coat in panko. Set on lined baking sheet and repeat with the remaining dough.
8. In a small saucepan, heat the remaining 1 to 2 cups of olive oil, so that the oil is about 1 inch deep, over medium-high heat. The smaller the pan, the less oil you will need, but you will need more for each batch.
9. Test if the oil is ready by throwing a pinch of panko into pot. If it sizzles, the oil is ready for frying. If it sinks, it's not quite ready. Once the oil is heated, fry the croquettes 3 or 4 at a time, depending on the size of your pan, removing with a slotted spoon when golden brown. You will need to adjust the temperature of the oil occasionally to prevent burning. If the croquettes get dark brown very quickly, lower the temperature.

PER SERVING

Calories: 245 | Total Fat: 22g | Total Carbs: 7g | Net Carbs: 6g | Fiber: 1g | Protein: 6g | Sodium: 85mg

Shrimp In Creamy Pesto Over Zoodles

Prep time: 10 minutes | Cook time: 10 minutes | Serves 4

- 1 pound peeled and deveined fresh shrimp
- Salt
- Freshly ground black pepper
- 2 tablespoons extra-virgin olive oil
- ½ small onion, slivered
- 8 ounces store-bought jarred pesto
- ¾ cup crumbled goat or feta cheese, plus more for serving
- 6 cups Zucchini Noodles (from about 2 large zucchini), for serving
- ¼ cup chopped flat-leaf Italian parsley, for garnish

1. In a bowl, season the shrimp with salt and pepper and set aside.
2. In a large skillet, heat the olive oil over medium-high heat. Sauté the onion until just golden, 5 to 6 minutes.
3. Reduce the heat to low and add the pesto and cheese, whisking to combine and melt the cheese. Bring to a low simmer and add the shrimp. Reduce the heat back to low and cover. Cook until the shrimp is cooked through and pink, another 3 to 4 minutes.
4. Serve warm over Zucchini Noodles, garnishing with chopped parsley and additional crumbled cheese, if desired.

PER SERVING

Calories: 491 | Total Fat: 35g | Total Carbs: 15g | Net Carbs: 11g | Fiber: 4g | Protein: 29g | Sodium: 870mg

Spicy Blackened Tilapia Tacos with Slaw

Prep time: 20 minutes | Cook time: 3 minutes | Serves 4

- 1 tbsp olive oil
- 1 tsp chili powder
- 2 tilapia fillets
- 1 tsp paprika
- 4 keto tortillas
- Slaw:
- ½ cup red cabbage, shredded
- 1 tbsp lemon juice
- 1 tsp apple cider vinegar
- 1 tbsp olive oil

1. Season tilapia with chili powder and paprika. Heat the olive oil in a skillet over medium heat.
2. Add tilapia, and cook until blackened, about 3 minutes per side. Cut into strips. Divide the tilapia between the tortillas.
3. Combine all of the slaw ingredients in a bowl. Divide the slaw between the tortillas.

PER SERVING

Cal: 260 | Net Carbs: 3.5g | Fat: 20g | Protein 13.8g

Mustardy Crab Cakes

Prep time: 15 minutes | Cook time: 3 minutes |Serves 4

- 1 tbsp coconut oil
- 1 pound lump crab meat
- 1 tsp Dijon mustard
- 1 egg
- ¼ cup mayonnaise
- 1 tbsp coconut flour
- 1 tbsp cilantro, chopped

1. In a bowl, add crab meat, mustard, mayonnaise, coconut flour, egg, cilantro, salt, and pepper; mix to combine. Make patties out of the mixture. Melt coconut oil in a skillet over medium heat. Add crab patties and cook for 2-3 minutes per side. Remove to kitchen paper.
2. Serve.

PER SERVING

Cal: 315 | Fat: 24.5g | Net Carbs: 1.6g | Protein 15.3g

Coconut Fried Shrimp with Cilantro Sauce

Prep time: 15 minutes | Cook time: 9 minutes |Serves 4

- 2 tsp coconut flour
- 2 tbsp grated Pecorino cheese
- 1 egg, beaten in a bowl
- ¼ tsp curry powder
- 1 pound shrimp, shelled
- 3 tbsp coconut oil
- Salt to taste
- Sauce
- 2 tbsp ghee
- 2 tbsp cilantro leaves, chopped
- ½ onion, diced
- ½ cup coconut cream
- ½ ounce Paneer cheese, grated

1. Combine coconut flour, Pecorino cheese, curry powder, and salt in a bowl.
2. Melt the coconut oil in a skillet over medium heat. Dip the shrimp in the egg first, and then coat with the dry mixture. Fry until golden and crispy, about 5 minutes.
3. In another skillet, melt the ghee. Add onion and cook for 3 minutes. Add curry and cilantro and cook for 30 seconds. Stir in coconut cream and Paneer cheese and cook until thickened. Add the shrimp and coat well. Serve warm.

PER SERVING

Cal: 741 | Fat: 64g | Net Carbs: 4.3g | Protein 34.4g

Salmon Cakes with Avocado

Prep time: 15 minutes | Cook time: 15 minutes | Serves 4

- 1 (14.5-ounce) can red salmon or 1 pound wild-caught salmon filet, skin removed
- ½ cup minced red onion
- 1 large egg
- 2 tablespoons avocado oil mayonnaise, plus more for serving
- 1 very ripe avocado, pitted, peeled, and mashed
- ½ cup almond flour
- 1 to 2 teaspoons dried dill
- 1 teaspoon garlic powder
- 1 teaspoon salt
- ½ teaspoon paprika
- ½ teaspoon freshly ground black pepper
- Zest and juice of 1 lemon
- ¼ cup extra-virgin olive oil
- Roasted Garlic Aioli, for serving

1. Remove the spine, large bones, and pieces of skin from the salmon. Place the salmon and red onion in a large bowl and using a fork, break up any lumps.
2. Add the egg, mayonnaise, and avocado and combine well.
3. In a small bowl, whisk together the almond flour, dill, garlic powder, salt, paprika, and pepper.
4. Add the dry ingredients and lemon zest and juice to the salmon and combine well.
5. Form into 8 small patties, about 2 inches in diameter and place on a plate. Let rest for 15 minutes.
6. In a large cast iron skillet, heat the olive oil over medium heat. Fry the patties until browned, 2 to 3 minutes per side. Cover the skillet, reduce heat to low, and cook another 6 to 8 minutes, or until the cakes are set in the center. Remove from the skillet and serve warm with additional mayonnaise or Roasted Garlic Aioli.

PER SERVING

Calories: 343 | Total Fat: 26g | Total Carbs: 5g | Net Carbs: 4g | Fiber: 1g | Protein: 23g | Sodium: 696mg

Chimichurri Tiger Shrimp

Prep time: 55 minutes | Cook time: 32 minutes |Serves 4

- 1 pound tiger shrimp, peeled and deveined
- 2 tbsp olive oil
- 1 garlic clove, minced
- Juice of 1 lime
- Salt and black pepper to taste
- Chimichurri
- Salt and black pepper to taste
- ¼ cup extra-virgin olive oil
- 2 garlic cloves, minced
- 1 lime, juiced
- ¼ cup red wine vinegar
- 2 cups parsley, minced
- ¼ tsp red pepper flakes

1. Combine the shrimp, olive oil, garlic, and lime juice, in a bowl, and let marinate in the fridge for 30 minutes.
2. To make the chimichurri dressing, blitz the chimichurri ingredients in a blender until smooth; set aside.
3. Preheat your grill to medium. Add shrimp and cook about 2 minutes per side. Serve shrimp drizzled with the chimichurri dressing.

PER SERVING

Cal: 523 | Fat: 30.3g | Net Carbs: 7.2g | Protein 49g

Mussel Coconut Curry

Prep time: 25 minutes | Cook time: 10 minutes |Serves 4

- 2 tbsp cup coconut oil
- 2 green onions, chopped
- 1 lb mussels, cleaned, de-bearded
- 1 shallot, chopped
- 1 garlic clove, minced
- ½ cup coconut milk
- ½ cup white wine
- 1 tsp red curry powder
- 2 tbsp parsley, chopped

1. Cook the shallots and garlic in the wine over low heat. Stir in the coconut milk and red curry powder and cook for 3 minutes.
2. Add the mussels and steam for 7 minutes or until their shells are opened. Then, use a slotted spoon to remove to a bowl leaving the sauce in the pan. Discard any closed mussels at this point.
3. Stir the coconut oil into the sauce, turn the heat off, and stir in the parsley and green onions. Serve the sauce immediately with a butternut squash mash.

PER SERVING

Cal: 356 | Fat: 20.6g | Net Carbs: 0.3g | Protein 21.1g

Chapter 8
Sides & Snacks

Hot Chard Artichoke Dip

Prep time: 10 minutes | Cook time: 20 minutes | Serves 4

- 4 ounces cream cheese, at room temperature
- ½ cup coconut milk
- ½ cup grated Asiago cheese
- ½ cup shredded Cheddar cheese
- 1 teaspoon minced garlic
- Dash hot sauce (optional)
- 2 cups chopped Swiss chard
- ½ cup roughly chopped artichoke hearts (packed in brine, not oil)

1. Preheat the oven. Set the oven temperature to 450°F.
2. Mix the ingredients. In a large bowl, stir together the cream cheese, coconut milk, Asiago, Cheddar, garlic, and hot sauce (if using), until everything is well mixed. Stir in the chard and the artichoke hearts and mix until they're well incorporated. Note: You've got to use artichokes packed in brine rather than oil because the extra oil will come out of the dip when you heat it, which will mess up the texture.
3. Bake. Spoon the mixture into a 1-quart baking dish, and bake it for 15 to 20 minutes until it's bubbly and lightly golden.
4. Serve. Cut up low-carb veggies to serve with this creamy, rich dip.

PER SERVING

Calories: 280 | Total Fat: 25g | Total Carbs: 5g | Fiber: 1g | Net Carbs: 4g | Sodium: 411mg | Protein: 11g

Cheese Almond Crackers

Prep time: 10 minutes | Cook time: 20 minutes | Serves 4

- Olive oil cooking spray
- 1 cup almond flour
- ½ cup finely shredded Cheddar cheese
- 1 tablespoon nutritional yeast
- ¼ teaspoon baking soda
- ¼ teaspoon garlic powder
- ¼ teaspoon sea salt
- 1 egg
- 2 teaspoons good-quality olive oil

1. Preheat the oven. Set the oven temperature to 350°F. Line a baking sheet with parchment paper and set it aside. Lightly grease two sheets of parchment paper with olive oil cooking spray and set them aside.
2. Mix the dry ingredients. In a large bowl, stir together the almond flour, Cheddar, nutritional yeast, baking soda, garlic powder, and salt until everything is well blended.
3. Mix the wet ingredients. In a small bowl, whisk together the egg and olive oil. Using a wooden spoon, mix the wet ingredients into the dry until the dough sticks together to form a ball. Gather the ball together using your hands, and knead it firmly a few times.
4. Roll out the dough. Place the ball on one of the lightly greased parchment paper pieces and press it down to form a disk. Place the other piece of greased parchment paper on top and use a rolling pin to roll the dough into a 9-by-12-inch rectangle about ⅛ inch thick.
5. Cut the dough. Use a pizza cutter and a ruler to cut the edges of the dough into an even rectangle and cut the dough into 1½-by-1½-inch columns and rows. Transfer the crackers to the baking sheet.
6. Bake. Bake the crackers for 15 to 20 minutes until they're crisp. Transfer them to a wire rack and let them cool completely.
7. Serve. Eat the crackers immediately or store them in an airtight container in the refrigerator for up to one week.

PER SERVING

Calories: 146 | Total Fat: 12g | Total Carbs: 1g | Fiber: 1g | Net Carbs: 0g | Sodium: 105mg | Protein: 7g

Greek Deviled Eggs

Prep time: 15 minutes | Cook time: 15 minutes | Serves 4

- 4 large hardboiled eggs
- 2 tablespoons Roasted Garlic Aioli or whole-milk Greek yogurt
- ½ cup finely crumbled feta cheese
- 8 pitted Kalamata olives, finely chopped
- 2 tablespoons chopped sun-dried tomatoes
- 1 tablespoon minced red onion
- ½ teaspoon dried dill
- ¼ teaspoon freshly ground black pepper

1. Slice the hardboiled eggs in half lengthwise, remove the yolks, and place the yolks in a medium bowl. Reserve the egg white halves and set aside.
2. Smash the yolks well with a fork. Add the aioli, feta, olives, sun-dried tomatoes, onion, dill, and pepper and stir to combine until smooth and creamy.
3. Spoon the filling into each egg white half and chill for 30 minutes, or up to 24 hours, covered.

PER SERVING

Calories: 147 | Total Fat: 11g | Total Carbs: 3g | Net Carbs: 3g | Fiber: 0g | Protein: 9g | Sodium: 334mg

Coconut Creamed Spinach

Prep time: 10 minutes | Cook time: 20 minutes | Serves 4

- 1 tablespoon grass-fed butter
- ¼ onion, thinly sliced
- 4 cups coarsely chopped spinach, thoroughly washed
- ½ cup vegetable broth
- ¼ cup coconut cream
- ⅛ teaspoon ground nutmeg
- Pinch sea salt
- Pinch freshly ground black pepper

1. Cook the onion. In a large skillet over medium heat, melt the butter. Add the onion and sauté until it's softened, about 2 minutes.
2. Cook the spinach. Stir in the spinach, vegetable broth, coconut cream, nutmeg, salt, and pepper and cook, giving it a stir from time to time, until the spinach is tender and the sauce thickens, about 15 minutes.
3. Serve. Put the creamed spinach in a bowl and serve.

PER SERVING

Calories: 85 | Total Fat: 8g | Total Carbs: 3g | Fiber: 1g | Net Carbs: 2g | Sodium: 61mg | Protein: 1g

Simple Butter Sautéed Vegetables

Prep time: 10 minutes | Cook time: 10 minutes | Serves 4

- 2 tablespoons grass-fed butter
- 1 tablespoon good-quality olive oil
- 2 teaspoons minced garlic
- 2 zucchini, cut into ¼-inch rounds
- 1 red bell pepper, cut into thick slices
- 1 yellow bell pepper, cut into thick slices
- Sea salt, for seasoning
- Freshly ground black pepper, for seasoning

1. Cook the vegetables. In a large skillet over medium-high heat, warm the butter and olive oil. Add the garlic and sauté it for 2 minutes. Add the zucchini and the red and yellow bell peppers to the skillet and sauté, stirring from time to time, for 7 minutes.
2. Serve. Season the vegetables with salt and pepper, spoon them into a bowl, and serve.

PER SERVING

Calories: 100 | Total Fat: 9g | Total Carbs: 4g | Fiber: 1g | Net Carbs: 3g | Sodium: 67mg | Protein: 1g

Strawberry Rhubarb Scones

Prep time:10 minutes | Cook time:30 minutes | Serves 10

- For The Scones
- 4 tablespoons (½ stick) unsalted butter, melted, plus more for greasing
- ½ cup granulated erythritol–monk fruit blend
- 3 large eggs
- ½ cup full-fat sour cream
- 1½ cups finely milled almond flour, sifted
- ½ cup coconut flour
- 1½ teaspoons baking powder
- ¼ teaspoon sea salt
- ¾ cup fresh or frozen strawberries, thinly sliced
- ¾ cup fresh or frozen rhubarb, thinly sliced
- For The Icing
- ½ cup confectioners' erythritol–monk fruit blend
- ½ teaspoon vanilla extract
- 3 to 4 tablespoons heavy (whipping) cream

TO MAKE THE SCONES

1. Preheat the oven to 375°F. Grease the cast-iron skillet with butter and set aside.
2. In the large bowl, using an electric mixer on medium high, blend the granulated erythritol–monk fruit blend, melted butter, and eggs, stopping and scraping the bowl once or twice, as needed. Add the sour cream and mix well. Add the almond flour, coconut flour, baking powder, and salt, then stir until fully combined. Fold the strawberries and rhubarb into the batter.
3. Spread the batter evenly into the cast-iron skillet. Bake for 25 to 30 minutes, or until an inserted toothpick comes out clean. Cool completely, about 20 minutes.

TO MAKE THE ICING

1. In a small bowl, combine the confectioners' erythritol–monk fruit blend and vanilla. Add the heavy cream, starting with 1 tablespoon. Drizzle the icing onto the cooled scones and cut into 10 wedges before serving.
2. Store leftovers in an airtight container in the refrigerator for up to 5 days or freeze without the icing for up to 3 weeks.

PER SERVING

Calories: 222 | Total Fat: 20g | Total Carbohydrates: 6g | Net Carbs: 3g | Fiber: 3g | Protein: 6g |Sweetener: 19g

Citrus Marinated Olives

Prep time: 10 minutes | Cook time: 5 minutes | Serves 2

- 2 cups mixed green olives with pits
- ¼ cup red wine vinegar
- ¼ cup extra-virgin olive oil
- 4 garlic cloves, finely minced
- Zest and juice of 2 clementines or 1 large orange
- 1 teaspoon red pepper flakes
- 2 bay leaves
- ½ teaspoon ground cumin
- ½ teaspoon ground allspice

1. In a large glass bowl or jar, combine the olives, vinegar, oil, garlic, orange zest and juice, red pepper flakes, bay leaves, cumin, and allspice and mix well.
2. Cover and refrigerate for at least 4 hours or up to a week to allow the olives to marinate, tossing again before serving.

PER SERVING

Calories: 133 | Total Fat: 14g | Total Carbs: 3g | Net Carbs: 1g | Fiber: 2g | Protein: 1g | Sodium: 501mg

---

Warm Herbed Olives

Prep time: 5 minutes | Cook time: 4 minutes | Serves 4

- ¼ cup good-quality olive oil
- 4 ounces green olives
- 4 ounces Kalamata olives
- ½ teaspoon dried thyme
- ¼ teaspoon fennel seeds
- Pinch red pepper flakes

1. Sauté the olives. In a large skillet over medium heat, warm the olive oil. Sauté the olives, thyme, fennel seeds, and red pepper flakes until the olives start to brown, 3 to 4 minutes.
2. Serve. Put the olives into a bowl and serve them warm.

PER SERVING

Calories: 165 | Total Fat: 17g | Total Carbs: 3g | Fiber: 1g | Net Carbs: 2g | Sodium: 503mg | Protein: 1g

Blueberry Muffins

Prep time:5 minutes | Cook time:25 minutes | Serves 12

FOR THE MUFFINS

- Unsalted butter, for greasing
- 4 ounces full-fat cream cheese, at room temperature
- ¼ cup coconut oil, solid
- 1 cup plus 2 tablespoons granulated erythritol–monk fruit blend; less sweet: ¾ cup
- 4 large eggs, at room temperature
- 1¼ cups finely milled almond flour, sifted
- 1 teaspoon baking powder
- ½ teaspoon vanilla extract
- ¼ teaspoon sea salt
- 1 cup fresh or frozen blueberries
- For The Icing
- ¼ cup confectioners' erythritol–monk fruit blend
- ¼ teaspoon lemon extract
- 2 to 3 tablespoons heavy (whipping) cream

TO MAKE THE MUFFINS

1. Preheat the oven to 350°F. Grease the muffin pan generously with butter and set aside.
2. In the large bowl, using an electric mixer on high, beat the cream cheese and coconut oil for 1 to 2 minutes, stopping and scraping the bowl once or twice, as needed, until light and fluffy. Add the granulated erythritol–monk fruit blend and continue to mix well. Add the eggs, one at a time, mixing well after each addition.
3. Stir in the almond flour, baking powder, vanilla, and salt and mix well. Fold in the blueberries and mix until the batter is fully incorporated.
4. Pour the batter evenly into the prepared muffin cups and bake for 20 to 25 minutes, or until a toothpick inserted into the center of a muffin comes out clean. Allow to cool for 15 to 20 minutes.

TO MAKE THE ICING

1. In a small bowl, combine the confectioners' erythritol–monk fruit blend and lemon extract. Add the heavy cream, starting with 1 tablespoon. Add additional cream if the icing is too thick. Once the muffins have fully cooled, drizzle with icing.
2. Store leftovers in an airtight container in the refrigerator for up to 5 days or freeze without the glaze for up to 3 weeks.

PER SERVING

Calories: 177 | Total Fat: 16g | Total Carbohydrates: 5g | Net Carbs: 3g | Fiber: 2g | Protein: 5g | Sweetener: 20g

Buffalo Cauliflower Bites

Prep time: 10 minutes | Cook time: 20 minutes | Serves 4

- ¾ cup hot sauce, divided
- ½ cup chicken stock
- 2 tablespoons grass-fed butter, melted
- 1 tablespoon coconut flour
- 1 head cauliflower, cut into small florets

1. Preheat the oven. Set the oven temperature to 450°F. Line a baking sheet with parchment paper.
2. Prepare the sauce. In a large bowl, whisk together the hot sauce, chicken stock, melted butter, and coconut flour until everything is well blended.
3. Prepare the cauliflower. Add the cauliflower florets to the sauce and stir to get them completely coated with sauce.
4. Bake and serve. Spread the cauliflower on the baking sheet and bake until it's tender, about 20 minutes. Put the cauliflower in a bowl and serve.

PER SERVING

Calories: 94 | Total Fat: 8g | Total Carbs: 5g | Fiber: 2g | Net Carbs: 3g | Sodium: 1244mg | Protein: 3g

Tender Grilled Asparagus Spears

Prep time: 5 minutes | Cook time: 5 minutes | Serves 4

- 1 pound fresh asparagus spears, woody ends snapped off
- 2 tablespoons good-quality olive oil
- Sea salt, for seasoning
- Freshly ground black pepper, for seasoning

1. Preheat the grill. Set the grill to high heat.
2. Prepare the asparagus. In a medium bowl, toss the asparagus spears with the olive oil and season them with salt and pepper.
3. Grill and serve. Grill the asparagus until tender, 2 to 4 minutes. Arrange them on a platter and serve.

PER SERVING

Calories: 82 | Total Fat: 7g | Total Carbs: 5g | Fiber: 2g | Net Carbs: 3g | Sodium: 27mg | Protein: 2g

Dairy Free Chocolate Donuts

Prep time:10 minutes | Cook time:30 minutes | Serves 12

- For The Donuts
- ¼ cup coconut oil, melted, plus more for greasing
- 2 cups granulated erythritol–monk fruit blend
- 2 cups finely milled almond flour, sifted
- ¾ cup coconut flour
- ¾ cup unsweetened cocoa powder
- 1½ teaspoons baking powder
- 1½ teaspoons baking soda
- ½ teaspoon sea salt
- 1 cup full-fat coconut milk or almond milk
- 1 cup boiling water
- 1 teaspoon vanilla extract
- 3 large eggs
- For The Icing
- 4 ounces unsweetened baking chocolate, coarsely chopped
- ½ cup confectioners' erythritol–monk fruit blend
- 2 tablespoons coconut oil
- ¼ teaspoon sea salt

TO MAKE THE DONUTS

1. Preheat the oven to 350°F. Grease the silicone molds well with coconut oil.
2. In the large bowl, combine the granulated erythritol–monk fruit blend, almond flour, coconut flour, cocoa powder, baking powder, baking soda, and salt. Add the coconut milk, boiling water, coconut oil, and vanilla. Add the eggs, one at a time, mixing well after each addition. Using an electric mixer on medium, mix the batter until fully incorporated, stopping and scraping the bowl once or twice, as needed.
3. Pour the batter into the prepared molds and bake for 25 to 30 minutes, until a toothpick inserted in a donut comes out clean. Allow to fully cool, 15 to 20 minutes, before taking the donuts out of the molds.

TO MAKE THE ICING

1. Line the baking sheet with parchment paper and set aside.
2. In the small microwave-safe bowl, melt the baking chocolate in the microwave in 30-second intervals. Add the confectioners' erythritol–monk fruit blend, coconut oil, and salt and combine until silky smooth.
3. Once the donuts are fully cooled, dip each of them into the chocolate icing, taking care to evenly coat the tops. Place them on the prepared baking sheet and allow them to chill in the refrigerator until ready to serve.
4. Store leftovers in an airtight container in the refrigerator for up to 5 days.

PER SERVING

Calories: 309 | Total Fat: 28g | Total Carbohydrates: 11g | Net Carbs: 5g | Fiber: 6g | Protein: 8g |Sweetener: 40g

Olive Tapenade with Anchovies

Prep time: 10 minutes | Cook time: 5 minutes | Serves 2

- 2 cups pitted Kalamata olives or other black olives
- 2 anchovy fillets, chopped
- 2 teaspoons chopped capers
- 1 garlic clove, finely minced
- 1 cooked egg yolk
- 1 teaspoon Dijon mustard
- ¼ cup extra-virgin olive oil
- Seedy Crackers, Versatile Sandwich Round, or vegetables, for serving (optional)

1. Rinse the olives in cold water and drain well.
2. In a food processor, blender, or a large jar (if using an immersion blender) place the drained olives, anchovies, capers, garlic, egg yolk, and Dijon. Process until it forms a thick paste.
3. with the food processor running, slowly stream in the olive oil.
4. Transfer to a small bowl, cover, and refrigerate at least 1 hour to let the flavors develop. Serve with Seedy Crackers, atop a Versatile Sandwich Round, or with your favorite crunchy vegetables.

PER SERVING

Calories: 179 | Total Fat: 19g | Total Carbs: 3g | Net Carbs: 1g | Fiber: 2g | Protein: 2g | Sodium: 812mg

Crispy Grilled Kale Leaves

Prep time: 10 minutes | Cook time: 5 minutes | Serves 4

- ½ cup good-quality olive oil
- 2 teaspoons freshly squeezed lemon juice
- ½ teaspoon garlic powder
- 7 cups large kale leaves, thoroughly washed and patted dry
- Sea salt, for seasoning
- Freshly ground black pepper, for seasoning

1. Preheat the grill. Set the grill to medium-high heat.
2. Mix the dressing. In a large bowl, whisk together the olive oil, lemon juice, and garlic powder until it thickens.
3. Prepare the kale. Add the kale leaves to the bowl and use your fingers to massage the dressing thoroughly all over the leaves. Season the leaves lightly with salt and pepper.
4. Grill and serve. Place the kale leaves in a single layer on the preheated grill. Grill for 1 to 2 minutes, turn the leaves over, and grill the other side for 1 minute, until they're crispy. Put the leaves on a platter and serve.

PER SERVING

Calories: 282 | Total Fat: 28g | Total Carbs: 9g | Fiber: 3g | Net Carbs: 6g | Sodium: 37mg | Protein: 3g

Nut-Free Pumpkin Bread

Prep time:15 minutes | Cook time:55 minutes | Serves 12

- 4 tablespoons (½ stick) unsalted butter, melted, plus more for greasing
- 1 cup granulated erythritol–monk fruit blend; less sweet: ½ cup
- ¾ cup canned pumpkin puree
- 1 teaspoon vanilla extract
- 4 large eggs, at room temperature
- 1½ cups sunflower seed flour
- ½ cup golden flaxseed meal, reground in a clean coffee grinder
- 1½ teaspoons baking powder
- 1 tablespoon psyllium husk powder
- 2 teaspoons ground cinnamon
- 1½ teaspoons ground ginger
- ½ teaspoon ground nutmeg
- ¼ teaspoon ground cloves
- ¼ teaspoon sea salt

1. Preheat the oven to 350°F. Grease the loaf pan with butter and set aside.
2. In the large bowl, using an electric mixer on medium high, beat the butter, erythritol–monk fruit blend, pumpkin puree, and vanilla until well blended, stopping and scraping the bowl once or twice, as needed. Add the eggs, one at time, stopping and scraping the bowl once or twice, as needed. Add the sunflower seed flour, flaxseed meal, baking powder, psyllium husk powder, cinnamon, ginger, nutmeg, cloves, and salt.
3. Spread the batter into the prepared loaf pan. Bake for 40 to 55 minutes, or until a toothpick inserted into the center comes out clean. Let cool for 10 minutes in the pan.
4. Remove the pumpkin bread from the pan and allow to cool 15 to 20 minutes.
5. Store leftovers in an airtight container in the refrigerator for up to 5 days or freeze for 3 weeks.

PER SERVING

Calories: 195 | Total Fat: 17g | Total Carbohydrates: 7g | Net Carbs: 3g | Fiber: 4g | Protein: 6g | Sweetener: 12g

Classic Cheesecake

Prep time:15 minutes | Cook time:1 hour 30 minutes | Serves 14

FOR THE CRUST

- 8 tablespoons (1 stick) unsalted butter, melted, plus more for greasing
- 2 cups finely milled almond flour
- ½ cup granulated erythritol–monk fruit blend
- ½ teaspoon sea salt
- For The Cheesecake
- 32 ounces full-fat cream cheese, at room temperature
- 1½ cups granulated erythritol–monk fruit blend
- 4 large eggs
- 16 ounces full-fat sour cream
- 1 teaspoon vanilla extract
- ¼ teaspoon sea salt
- Unsalted butter, for greasing
- For The Sour Cream Topping
- 1½ cups sour cream
- 3 tablespoons granulated erythritol–monk fruit blend
- ½ teaspoon vanilla extract

TO MAKE THE CRUST

1. Preheat the oven to 350°F. Lightly grease the bottom of the springform pan with butter.
2. In the medium bowl, mix the almond flour, erythritol–monk fruit blend, and salt and combine well. Add the melted butter and mix until fully incorporated. Once combined, add the mixture to the bottom of the springform pan. Use the bottom of a glass cup to press the mixture evenly into the pan.
3. Bake the crust for 20 to 25 minutes, until lightly browned. Move the crust to the cooling rack and allow the crust to cool for 15 to 20 minutes. Leave the oven on and reduce the oven temperature to 325°F.

TO MAKE THE CHEESECAKE

1. In the large bowl, using an electric mixer on high, beat the cream cheese and erythritol–monk fruit blend until well incorporated. Reduce the speed to medium low and add the eggs, one at a time, stopping and scraping the bowl once or twice, as needed. Add the sour cream, vanilla, and salt. Combine the mixture until fully incorporated and velvety smooth. This may take up to 5 minutes. Stop and scrape the bowl a couple of times during this process as well.
2. Use butter to lightly grease the sides of the cooled springform pan with the crust. Pour the cheesecake batter into the almond crust and spread evenly. Wrap the bottom and sides of the springform pan with heavy-duty aluminum foil. Put the wrapped springform pan in a roasting pan large enough to accommodate the springform pan without touching the sides.
3. Put the roasting pan in the oven and carefully pour in boiling water to halfway up the sides of the springform pan. Bake for 1 hour to 1 hour 10 minutes, until the cheesecake is set around the edges but the center jiggles.
4. Allow the cheesecake to cool in the oven for 1 hour with the oven off and door slightly ajar.
5. Move the cheesecake to the cooling rack to further cool on the kitchen counter for at least 1 additional hour. Once fully cooled, run a knife around the sides of the springform pan to release the cheesecake.
6. Carefully wrap the cheesecake with plastic wrap and chill in the refrigerator for at least 12 hours and up to 36 hours before serving.

TO MAKE THE SOUR CREAM TOPPING

1. In the small bowl, combine the sour cream, erythritol–monk fruit blend, and vanilla. Spread evenly on top of the cheesecake right before serving, cut into 14 slices, and serve.
2. Store leftovers in an airtight container in the refrigerator for up to 5 days.

PER SERVING

Calories: 413 | Total Fat: 41g | Total Carbohydrates: 4g | Net Carbs: 4g | Fiber: 0g | Protein: 7g |Sweetener: 30g

Thai Noodle Salad

Prep time: 10 minutes | Cook time:5 minutes |Serves 4

- 1 cup shredded purple cabbage
- 1 cup shredded green cabbage
- ¼ cup chopped scallions
- ¼ cup chopped fresh cilantro
- 3 cups shirataki noodles, rinsed and drained
- ½ cup chopped cashews
- 2 tablespoons minced garlic
- 2 tablespoons minced fresh ginger
- ½ cup water
- 1 tablespoon freshly squeezed lime juice
- 1 tablespoon soy sauce
- 1 tablespoon coconut aminos
- ⅓ cup creamy natural cashew butter
- ½ teaspoon salt
- Liquid stevia

1. In a large bowl, combine the purple and green cabbage, scallions, cilantro, noodles, and cashews.
2. In a medium bowl, combine the garlic, ginger, water, lime juice, soy sauce, coconut aminos, cashew butter, and salt. Sweeten with stevia as desired. Mix well with a whisk until thoroughly combined.
3. Pour the dressing over the vegetable and noodle mixture, then toss well.
4. Divide into 4 equal servings.

PER SERVING

Calories: 295 | Fat: 19g | Protein: 8g | Total Carbs: 23g | Net Carbs: 17g | Fiber: 6g | Sugar: 4g | Sodium: 532mg | Macros: Fat: 58% | Protein: 11% | Carbs: 31%

Burrata Caprese Stack

Prep time: 5 minutes | Cook time: 5 minutes | Serves 4

- 1 large organic tomato, preferably heirloom
- ½ teaspoon salt
- ¼ teaspoon freshly ground black pepper
- 1 (4-ounce) ball burrata cheese
- 8 fresh basil leaves, thinly sliced
- 2 tablespoons extra-virgin olive oil
- 1 tablespoon red wine or balsamic vinegar

1. Slice the tomato into 4 thick slices, removing any tough center core and sprinkle with salt and pepper. Place the tomatoes, seasoned-side up, on a plate.
2. On a separate rimmed plate, slice the burrata into 4 thick slices and place one slice on top of each tomato slice. Top each with one-quarter of the basil and pour any reserved burrata cream from the rimmed plate over top.
3. Drizzle with olive oil and vinegar and serve with a fork and knife.

PER SERVING

Calories: 153 | Total Fat: 13g | Total Carbs: 2g | Net Carbs: 1g | Fiber: 1g | Protein: 7g | Sodium: 469mg

Crab Stuffed Mushrooms

Prep time: 10 minutes | Cook time: 20 minutes | Serves 4

- 1 cup cooked chopped crab
- 1 cup cream cheese, softened
- ½ cup grated Parmesan cheese
- ¼ cup ground almonds
- 1 scallion, chopped
- 1 tablespoon chopped fresh parsley
- 1 teaspoon minced garlic
- 12 large button mushrooms, cleaned and stemmed
- Olive oil cooking spray

1. Preheat the oven. Set the oven temperature to 375°F. Line a baking sheet with parchment paper.
2. Mix the filling. In a large bowl, stir together the crab, cream cheese, Parmesan, almonds, scallion, parsley, and garlic until everything is well mixed.
3. Precook the mushrooms. Place the mushrooms stem-side up on the baking sheet and lightly spray them with olive oil. Bake them for 2 minutes then drain them stem-side down on paper towels.
4. Stuff the mushrooms. Turn the mushrooms over and place them back on the baking sheet. Spoon about 1½ tablespoons of the filling into each mushroom.
5. Bake the mushrooms. Bake for 15 minutes until the mushrooms are lightly golden and bubbly.
6. Serve. Arrange the mushrooms on a serving platter.

PER SERVING

Calories: 300 | Total Fat: 25g | Total Carbs: 4g | Fiber: 0g | Net Carbs: 4g | Sodium: 554mg | Protein: 16g

County Fair Cinnamon Donuts

Prep time: 10 minutes | Cook time: 25 minutes |Serves 6

- 11½ ounces cream cheese (1 cup plus 7 tablespoons), room temperature
- ½ cup extra-virgin olive oil
- ¼ cup heavy whipping cream
- 4 large eggs
- ½ teaspoon liquid stevia
- ½ teaspoon maple extract
- ½ teaspoon vanilla extract
- ¼ cup plus 2 tablespoons coconut flour
- 2 teaspoons ground cinnamon
- 1 teaspoon baking powder
- 1 teaspoon xanthan gum
- ¼ teaspoon pink Himalayan salt
- Topping:
- ¼ cup granular erythritol
- ¼ cup ground cinnamon
- Special Equipment:
- 6-cavity silicone donut pan

1. Preheat the oven to 400°F and grease a 6-cavity donut pan with coconut oil spray.
2. In a large bowl, beat the cream cheese, olive oil, cream, eggs, stevia, and extracts using a hand mixer until smooth and fully incorporated. Set aside.
3. In a small bowl, whisk together the coconut flour, cinnamon, baking powder, xanthan gum, and salt using a whisk. Add the dry mixture to the wet ingredients and combine using the hand mixer. Fill the greased cavities of the donut mold to the brim, making sure not to overfill.
4. Bake for 25 minutes, until the donuts are puffed up and a toothpick comes out clean.
5. Meanwhile, put the ingredients for the topping on a plate and combine using your fingers. After removing the donuts from the oven, allow to cool in the pan for 5 minutes, then toss them, one at a time, in the cinnamon-sugar mixture. Set the coated donuts on a wire baking rack to cool for an additional 10 minutes prior to eating.
6. Store leftovers in a sealed container in the refrigerator for up to 4 days.

PER SERVING

Calories: 461 | Fat: 44.8 g | Protein: 8.7 g | Carbs: 6.8g | Fiber: 2.5 g | Sugar Alcohol: 8g

Dairy-Free Cranberry Muffins

Prep time:10 minutes | Cook time:25 minutes | Serves 12

- ½ cup coconut oil, solid, plus more for greasing
- ¾ cup granulated erythritol–monk fruit blend
- 2 large eggs, at room temperature
- ¼ cup coconut or almond milk
- ½ teaspoon orange extract
- 1½ cups finely milled almond flour, sifted
- 1¼ teaspoons baking powder
- 1 teaspoon ground cinnamon
- ¼ teaspoon ground nutmeg
- ¼ teaspoon sea salt
- 1 cup fresh or frozen cranberries

1. Preheat the oven 350°F. Grease the muffin pan generously with coconut oil and set aside.
2. In a large bowl, using an electric mixer on medium high, cream the coconut oil and erythritol–monk fruit blend for 1 to 2 minutes, stopping and scraping the bowl once or twice, as needed, until light and fluffy. Beat in the eggs, one at a time. Add the coconut milk and orange extract and combine well.
3. In another large bowl, combine the almond flour, baking powder, cinnamon, nutmeg, and salt. Add the dry ingredients to the wet ingredients and mix well. Fold in the cranberries.
4. Pour the batter evenly into the muffin cups. Bake for 20 to 25 minutes, or until a toothpick inserted in a muffin comes out clean. Allow to cool for 15 to 20 minutes before serving.
5. Store in an airtight container in the refrigerator for up to 5 days or freeze for up to 3 weeks.

PER SERVING

Calories: 173 | Total Fat: 17g | Total Carbohydrates: 4g | Net Carbs: 2g | Fiber: 2g | Protein: 4g |Sweetener: 12g

Blackberry Mini Cheesecakes

Prep time: 10 minutes | Cook time: 13 minutes |Serves 8

CRUST:

- 2½ ounces raw walnuts
- 3 tablespoons unsalted butter
- 1 large egg yolk
- ¼ teaspoon plus 10 drops of liquid stevia
- ¼ teaspoon pink Himalayan salt

FILLING:

- 12 ounces cream cheese (1½ cups), room temperature
- ¼ cup plus 2 tablespoons sour cream
- ¾ cup heavy whipping cream
- ¾ cup powdered erythritol
- 3½ ounces fresh blackberries (about ¾ cup), halved, plus extra whole berries for garnish

1. Make the crust: Put all the crust ingredients in a food processor and process until finely chopped and fully combined. Divide the crust mixture

between two 4-inch springform pans. Using a rubber spatula, flatten the crusts to cover the bottoms of the pans. Place in the freezer to chill for 30 minutes.
2. Preheat the oven to 325°F. Bake the chilled crusts for 13 minutes, or until slightly browned. Allow to cool completely before adding the filling.
3. Make the filling: Put the cream cheese, sour cream, and heavy cream in a large mixing bowl and combine using a hand mixer until the mixture has a thick, creamy consistency. Add the erythritol and mix to combine.
4. Fold in the halved blackberries. Pour the filling over the cooled crusts and use a rubber spatula to spread the filling evenly.
5. Freeze for at least 2½ hours or refrigerate for at least 6 hours prior to unmolding and serving. If you freeze the cheesecakes, allow them to sit out at room temperature for 10 minutes prior to serving. Garnish each cake with a few blackberries. To serve, cut each cheesecake into quarters, yielding a total of 8 servings.
6. Store leftovers in a sealed container in the refrigerator for up to a week.

PER SERVING

Calories: 482 | Fat: 48.5 g | Protein: 7.5 g | Carbs: 7.3g | Fiber: 1.7 g | Sugar Alcohol: 24g

Sautéed Wild Mushrooms with Bacon

Prep time: 10 minutes | Cook time: 15 minutes | Serves 4

- 6 strips uncured bacon, chopped
- 4 cups sliced wild mushrooms
- 2 teaspoons minced garlic
- 2 tablespoons chicken stock
- 1 tablespoon chopped fresh thyme

1. Cook the bacon. In a large skillet over medium-high heat, cook the bacon until it's crispy and cooked through, about 7 minutes.
2. Cook the mushrooms. Add the mushrooms and garlic and sauté until the mushrooms are tender, about 7 minutes.
3. Deglaze the pan. Add the chicken stock and stir to scrape up any browned bits in the bottom of the pan.
4. Garnish and serve. Put the mushrooms in a bowl, sprinkle them with the thyme, and serve.

PER SERVING

Calories: 214 | Total Fat: 19g | Total Carbs: 4g | Fiber: 0g | Net Carbs: 4g | Sodium: 154mg | Protein: 7g

Chocolate Chip Scones

Prep time:10 minutes | Cook time:30 minutes | Serves 10

- 4 tablespoons (½ stick) unsalted butter, melted, plus more for greasing
- ½ cup granulated erythritol–monk fruit blend
- 3 large eggs
- ½ cup full-fat sour cream
- 1½ cups finely milled almond flour, sifted
- ½ cup coconut flour
- 1½ teaspoons baking powder
- ¼ teaspoon sea salt
- 4 ounces sugar-free chocolate chips
- 2 tablespoons confectioners' erythritol– monk fruit blend, for dusting (optional)

1. Preheat the oven to 375°F. Grease the cast-iron skillet with butter and set aside.
2. In the large bowl, using an electric mixer on medium high, mix the granulated erythritol–monk fruit blend, melted butter, and eggs until well combined, stopping and scraping the bowl once or twice, as needed. Add the sour cream and mix well. Add the almond flour, coconut flour, baking powder, and salt, then stir until fully combined. Fold the sugar-free chocolate chips into the batter.
3. Spread the batter evenly into the cast-iron skillet. Bake for 25 to 30 minutes, or until a toothpick inserted into the center comes out clean. Allow the scones to cool completely. Dust with confectioners' erythritol–monk fruit blend (if using) and cut into 10 wedges before serving.
4. Store leftovers in an airtight container in the refrigerator for up to 5 days or freeze for up to 3 weeks.

PER SERVING

Calories: 268 | Total Fat: 24g | Total Carbohydrates: 8g | Net Carbs: 4g | Fiber: 4g | Protein: 7g |Sweetener: 10g

Manchego Crackers

Prep time: 15 minutes | Cook time: 15 minutes | Serves 4

- 4 tablespoons butter, at room temperature
- 1 cup finely shredded Manchego cheese
- 1 cup almond flour
- 1 teaspoon salt, divided
- ¼ teaspoon freshly ground black pepper
- 1 large egg

1. Using an electric mixer, cream together the butter and shredded cheese until well combined and smooth.
2. In a small bowl, combine the almond flour with ½ teaspoon salt and pepper. Slowly add the almond flour mixture to the cheese, mixing constantly until the dough just comes together to form a ball.
3. Transfer to a piece of parchment or plastic wrap and roll into a cylinder log about 1½ inches thick. Wrap tightly and refrigerate for at least 1 hour.
4. Preheat the oven to 350°F. Line two baking

sheets with parchment paper or silicone baking mats.
5. To make the egg wash, in a small bowl, whisk together the egg and remaining ½ teaspoon salt.
6. Slice the refrigerated dough into small rounds, about ¼ inch thick, and place on the lined baking sheets.
7. Brush the tops of the crackers with egg wash and bake until the crackers are golden and crispy, 12 to 15 minutes. Remove from the oven and allow to cool on a wire rack.
8. Serve warm or, once fully cooled, store in an airtight container in the refrigerator for up to 1 week.

PER SERVING

Calories: 243 | Total Fat: 23g | Total Carbs: 2g | Net Carbs: 1g | Fiber: 1g | Protein: 8g | Sodium: 792mg

Coconut Chocolate Cookies

Prep time: 10 minutes | Cook time: 15 minutes |Serves 1

- ¼ cup (½ stick) unsalted butter, room temperature
- 1 ounce cream cheese (2 tablespoons), room temperature
- ¼ cup plus 2 tablespoons powdered erythritol
- 1 large egg
- ¼ cup heavy whipping cream
- ¼ cup coconut flour
- ¼ cup cocoa powder
- ½ teaspoon baking powder
- ¼ teaspoon pink Himalayan salt
- ½ cup unsweetened coconut flakes

1. Preheat the oven to 325°F and line 2 baking sheets with parchment paper.
2. In a large bowl, use a hand mixer to cream the butter, cream cheese, and erythritol until light and fluffy. Mix in the egg and cream. Set aside.
3. In a small bowl, whisk together the coconut flour, cocoa powder, baking powder, and salt. Add the dry mixture to the wet ingredients in 2 batches, mixing with the hand mixer after each addition until you achieve a soft, slightly crumbly consistency. Fold in the coconut flakes.
4. Using a cookie scoop or spoon, scoop 12 even-sized balls of the dough onto the lined baking sheets and flatten with a fork to the desired size. They will not spread in the oven. Bake for 15 minutes, or until slightly firm to touch. Allow to cool on the baking sheets for 20 minutes prior to handling or they will fall apart.
5. Store in a sealed container or zip-top plastic bag in the refrigerator for up to a week.

PER SERVING

Calories: 91 | Fat: 8.4 g | Protein: 1.4 g | Carbs: 3g | Fiber: 1.8 g | Sugar Alcohol: 5g

Chapter 9
Vegan & Vegetarian

Charred Broccoli Salad with Sardines

Prep time: 5 minutes | Cook time: 10 minutes |Serves 4

- pound broccoli florets
- 1/2 white onion, thinly sliced
- 1(4-ounce) cans sardines in oil, drained
- 2 tablespoons fresh lime juice
- 1 teaspoon stone-ground mustard

1. Heat a lightly greased cast-iron skillet over medium-high heat. Cook the broccoli florets for 5 to 6 minutes until charred; work in batches.
2. In salad bowls, place the charred broccoli with onion and sardines. Toss with the lime juice and mustard. Serve at room temperature. Bon appétit!

PER SERVING

Calories: 159 | Fat: 7.1g | Carbs: 5.7g | Protein: 17.8g | Fiber: 3g

Italian Style Asparagus with Cheese

Prep time: 5 minutes | Cook time: 10 minutes |Serves 2

- 1/2 pound asparagus spears, trimmed, cut into bite-sized pieces
- 1 teaspoon Italian spice blend
- 1/2 tablespoon lemon juice
- 1 tablespoon extra-virgin olive oil
- 4 tablespoons Romano cheese, freshly grated

1. Bring a saucepan of lightly salted water to a boil. Turn the heat to medium-low. Add the asparagus spears and cook approximately 3 minutes. Drain and transfer to a serving bowl.
2. Add the Italian spice blend, lemon juice, and extra-virgin olive oil; toss until well coated.
3. Top with Romano cheese and serve immediately. Bon appétit!

PER SERVING

Calories: 193 | Fat: 14.1g | Carbs: 5.6g | Protein: 11.5g | Fiber: 2.4g

Sunday Cauliflower and Ham Bake

Prep time: 5 minutes | Cook time: 10 minutes |Serves 6

- 1½ pounds cauliflower, broken into small florets
- 1/2 cup Greek-Style yogurt
- 4 eggs, beaten
- 6 ounces ham, diced
- 1 cup Swiss cheese, preferably freshly grated

1. Place the cauliflower into a deep saucepan; cover with water and bring to a boil over high heat; immediately reduce the heat to medium-low.
2. Let it simmer, covered, approximately 6 minutes. Drain and mash with a potato masher.
3. Add in the yogurt, eggs and ham; stir until everything is well combined and incorporated.
4. Scrape the mixture into a lightly greased casserole dish. Top with the grated Swiss cheese and transfer to a preheated at 390 degrees F oven.
5. Bake for 15 to 20 minutes or until cheese bubbles and browns. Bon appétit!

PER SERVING

Calories: 236 | Fat: 13.8g | Carbs: 7.2g | Protein: 20.3g | Fiber: 2.3g

Garlicky Sautéed Kale

Prep time: 5 minutes | Cook time: 20 minutes |Serves 3

- 1/2 tablespoon olive oil
- 1 teaspoon fresh garlic, chopped
- 9 ounces kale, torn into pieces
- 1/2 cup Cottage cheese, creamed
- 1/2 teaspoon sea salt

1. Heat the olive oil in a saucepan over a moderate flame. Now, cook the garlic until just tender and aromatic.
2. Then, stir in the kale and continue to cook for about 10 minutes until all liquid evaporates.
3. Fold in the Cottage cheese and salt; stir until everything is heated through. Enjoy!

PER SERVING

Calories: 93 | Fat: 4.4g | Carbs: 6.1g | Protein: 7.1g | Fiber: 2.7g

Cheesy Zucchini Casserole

Prep time: 5 minutes | Cook time: 50 minutes |Serves 4

- Nonstick cooking spray
- 2 cups zucchini, thinly sliced
- 2 tablespoons leeks, sliced
- Freshly ground black pepper, to taste
- 1/2 teaspoon dried basil
- 1/2 teaspoon dried oregano
- 1/2 cup Cheddar cheese, grated
- 1/4 cup heavy cream
- 4 tablespoons Parmesan cheese, freshly grated
- 1 tablespoon butter, room temperature
- 1 teaspoon fresh garlic, minced

1. Start by preheating your oven to 370 degrees F. Lightly grease a casserole dish with a nonstick cooking spray.
2. Place 1 cup of the zucchini slices in the dish; add 1 tablespoon of leeks; sprinkle with salt, pepper, basil, and oregano. Top with 1/4 cup of Cheddar cheese. Repeat the layers one more time.
3. Place in the preheated oven and bake for about 40 to 45 minutes until the edges are nicely browned. Sprinkle with chopped chives, if desired. Bon appétit!

PER SERVING

Calories: 155 | Fat: 12.9g | Carbs: 3.5g | Fiber: 0.8g | Protein: 7.6g

Classic Club Salad

Prep time: 10 minutes | Cook time:5 minutes |Serves 4

- 3 tablespoons sour cream
- 3 tablespoons veganaise
- ¾ teaspoon garlic powder
- 1 teaspoon dried parsley
- 1 tablespoon heavy (whipping) cream
- 4 cups coarsely chopped romaine lettuce
- 1 cup diced cucumber
- ½ cup halved cherry tomatoes
- 4 hardboiled eggs, chopped
- 4 ounces cheddar cheese, grated

1. In a small bowl, mix together the sour cream, veganaise, garlic powder, onion powder, and parsley.
2. Stir in the cream and set aside.
3. Build the salad by layering the lettuce, cucumber, tomatoes, eggs, and cheddar cheese.
4. Divide the salad into 4 servings and top with dressing.

PER SERVING

Calories: 293 | Fat: 24g | Protein: 14g | Total Carbs: 5g | Net Carbs: 4g | Fiber: 1g | Sugar: 2g | Sodium: 312mg | Macros: Fat: 74% | Protein: 19% | Carbs: 7%

Stuffed Peppers with Cauliflower and Cheese

Prep time: 5 minutes | Cook time: 45 minutes |Serves 6

- 2 tablespoons vegetable oil
- 2 tablespoons yellow onion, chopped
- 1 teaspoon fresh garlic, crushed
- 1/2 pound ground pork
- 1/2 pound ground turkey
- 1 cup cauliflower rice
- 1/2 teaspoon sea salt
- 1/4 teaspoon red pepper flakes, crushed
- 1/2 teaspoon ground black pepper
- 1 teaspoon dried parsley flakes
- 6 medium-sized bell peppers, deveined and cleaned
- 1/2 cup tomato sauce
- 1/2 cup Cheddar cheese, shredded

1. Heat the oil in a pan over medium flame. Once hot, sauté the onion and garlic for 2 to 3 minutes.
2. Add the ground meat and cook for 6 minutes longer or until it is nicely browned. Add cauliflower rice and seasoning. Continue to cook for a further 3 minutes.
3. Divide the filling between the prepared bell peppers. Cover with a piece of foil. Place the peppers in a baking pan; add tomato sauce.
4. Bake in the preheated oven at 380 degrees F for 20 minutes. Uncover, top with cheese, and bake for 10 minutes more. Bon appétit!

PER SERVING

Calories: 244 | Fat: 12.9g | Carbs: 3.2g | Fiber: 1g | Protein: 16.5g

The Easiest Mushroom Stroganoff Ever

Prep time: 5 minutes | Cook time: 15 minutes |Serves 3

- 2 tablespoons olive oil
- 1/2 shallot, diced
- 3 cloves garlic, chopped
- 12 ounces brown mushrooms, thinly sliced
- 2 cups tomato sauce

1. Heat the olive oil in a stockpot over medium-high heat. Then, sauté the shallot for about 3 minutes until tender and fragrant.
2. Now, stir in the garlic and mushrooms and cook them for 1 minute more until aromatic.
3. Fold in the tomato sauce and bring to a boil; turn the heat to medium-low, cover, and continue to simmer for 5 to 6 minutes.
4. Salt to taste and serve over cauliflower rice if desired. Enjoy!

PER SERVING

Calories: 138 | Fat: 9.2g | Carbs: 7.1g | Protein: 3.4g | Fiber: 1.8g

Summer Zucchini Slaw

Prep time: 5 minutes | Cook time:10 minutes |Serves 3

- 1 zucchini, shredded
- 1 yellow bell pepper, sliced
- 1 red onion, thinly sliced
- 2 tablespoons extra-virgin olive oil
- 1 tablespoon balsamic vinegar
- 1 teaspoon Dijon mustard
- 1/4 teaspoon cumin seeds
- 1/4 teaspoon ground black pepper
- Sea salt, to taste

1. Thoroughly combine all ingredients in a salad bowl.
2. Refrigerate for 1 hour before serving or serve right away. Enjoy!

PER SERVING

Calories: 96 | Fat: 9.4g | Carbs: 2.8g | Protein: 0.7g | Fiber: 0.4g

Taco Lettuce Cups
Prep time: 10 minutes | Cook time:5 minutes |Serves 4

- 2 cups meatless crumbles
- 1 tablespoon coconut oil
- 1 cup chopped onion
- 1 bell pepper, chopped
- ½ pound mushrooms, sliced
- 1 head butter lettuce, leaves removed
- ¼ cup chopped fresh cilantro
- ½ cup salsa
- 1 cup shredded cheddar cheese
- 1 avocado, diced

1. In a medium skillet over medium heat, cook the crumbles until thoroughly warmed. Remove them from the skillet and set aside.
2. In the same skillet, melt the coconut oil and sauté the onion, bell pepper, garlic, and mushrooms for 4 to 5 minutes. Remove from the heat and stir in the crumbles.
3. Divide the mixture equally between lettuce cups on four dishes.
4. Top the cups with the cilantro, salsa, cheddar cheese, and avocado.

PER SERVING

Calories: 370 | Fat: 22g | Protein: 23g | Total Carbs: 20g | Net Carbs: 14g | Fiber: 6g | Sugar: 6g | Sodium: 584mg | Macros: Fat: 54% | Protein: 25% | Carbs: 21%

Hearty Keto Chili
Prep time: 5 minutes | Cook time: 20 minutes |Serves 2

- 3 ounces bacon, diced
- 1 brown onion, chopped
- 2 cloves garlic, minced
- 3/4 pound brown mushrooms, sliced
- 3 tablespoons dry red wine
- 1/2 teaspoon freshly ground black pepper
- 1 teaspoon chili powder
- 2 bay laurels
- Sea salt, to taste

1. Heat a soup pot over a medium-high flame and fry the bacon; once the bacon is crisp, remove from the pot and reserve.
2. Now, cook the brown onion and garlic until they have softened or about 6 minutes. Stir in the mushrooms and sauté them for 3 to 4 minutes longer.
3. Turn the heat to simmer; add the other ingredients and continue to cook for 10 minutes more, until most of the cooking liquid has evaporated.
4. Ladle into bowls and top with the reserved bacon. Bon appétit!

PER SERVING

Calories: 159 | Fat: 11.3g | Carbs: 6g | Protein: 6.9g | Fiber: 1.3g

Avocado Salsa with Queso Fresco
Prep time: 5 minutes | Cook time: 5 minutes |Serves 4

- 2 tomatoes, diced
- 3 scallions, chopped
- 1 poblano pepper, chopped
- 1 garlic clove, minced
- 2 ripe avocados, peeled, pitted and diced
- 1 tablespoon extra-virgin olive oil
- 2 tablespoons fresh lime juice
- Sea salt and ground black pepper, to season
- 1/4 cup queso fresco, crumbled

1. Place the tomatoes, scallions, poblano pepper, garlic and avocado in a serving bowl. Drizzle olive oil and lime juice over everything.
2. Season with salt and black pepper.
3. To serve, top with crumbled queso fresco and enjoy!

PER SERVING

Calories: 188 | Fat: 16g | Carbs: 6.9g | Protein: 3.6g | Fiber: 4.2g

Roasted Cauliflower Lettuce Cups
Prep time: 10 minutes | Cook time:20 minutes |Serves 4

- Nonstick cooking spray
- 1 head cauliflower, chopped
- 1 tablespoon avocado oil
- ½ teaspoon minced garlic
- 2 tablespoons curry powder
- ½ teaspoon salt
- ¼ teaspoon freshly ground black pepper
- 4 butter lettuce leaves
- 2 avocados, sliced
- 4 tablespoons cashews
- 4 tablespoons ranch dressing

1. Preheat the oven to 425°F.
2. Grease a rimmed baking sheet with cooking spray and put the cauliflower florets on it.
3. Pour the avocado oil on the florets and toss to coat; then sprinkle the florets with the garlic, curry powder, salt, and pepper.
4. Roast for about 20 minutes, or until the tops of the florets are slightly browned.
5. Remove from the oven and allow to cool for 5 to 7 minutes.
6. Place a scoop of florets into each butter lettuce cup and top each with ¼ of the avocado slices.
7. Sprinkle each cup with 1 tablespoon of cashews and 1 tablespoon of ranch dressing.

PER SERVING

Calories: 349 | Fat: 29g | Protein: 5g | Total Carbs: 17g | Net Carbs: 8g | Fiber: 9g | Sugar: 3g | Sodium: 446mg | Macros: Fat: 75% | Protein: 6% | Carbs: 19%

Avocado Pesto Panini

Prep time: 5 minutes | Cook time:10 minutes |Serves 1

- 2 tablespoons grass-fed butter, at room temperature
- 2 slices Easy Keto Bread or store bought
- 1 tablespoon basil pesto
- 2 slices Gruyère cheese
- ½ medium avocado, sliced

1. Heat a small griddle over medium heat.
2. Spread the butter on one side of each slice of bread.
3. Place one piece of bread, butter-side down, on the griddle and then layer the pesto, cheese, and avocado on top.
4. Top the sandwich with the second slice of bread, butter-side up, and gently press down.
5. Allow to cook for 4 to 5 minutes; then flip carefully and cook for an additional 3 to 4 minutes, or until the bread is golden brown.

PER SERVING

Calories: 824 | Fat: 72g | Protein: 29g | Total Carbs: 15g | Net Carbs: 7g | Fiber: 8g | Sugar: 3g | Sodium: 480mg | Macros: Fat: 79% | Protein: 14% | Carbs: 7%

Spinach Avocado Salad

Prep time: 10 minutes | Cook time:5 minutes |Serves 2

- 1½ cups fresh spinach leaves
- 4 hardboiled eggs, chopped
- ¼ cup chopped carrots
- ¼ cup chopped cucumbers
- ½ avocado, sliced
- ¼ cup diced tomatoes
- 1 tablespoon olive oil
- 1 tablespoon balsamic vinegar
- Salt
- Freshly ground black pepper

1. Place the spinach in a serving dish.
2. Top with the eggs, carrots, cucumbers, avocado, and tomatoes.
3. In a small bowl, mix together the oil and vinegar.
4. Pour the dressing on the salad and season with salt and pepper as needed.

PER SERVING

Calories: 291 | Fat: 23g | Protein: 13g | Total Carbs: 8g | Net Carbs: 4g | Fiber: 4g | Sugar: 2g | Sodium: 233mg | Macros: Fat: 71% | Protein: 18% | Carbs: 11%

Greek Cottage Cheese Salad

Prep time: 5 minutes | Cook time:5 minutes |Serves 1

- 1 cup 4-percent cottage cheese
- ⅓ cup halved cherry tomatoes
- 1 tablespoon chopped scallion, white part only
- ⅓ cup peeled and diced cucumber
- 2 tablespoons olive oil
- ½ cup Kalamata olives
- Salt
- Freshly ground black pepper

1. In a serving bowl, mix together the cottage cheese, cherry tomatoes, scallion, cucumber, olive oil, and olives, and season with salt and pepper as needed.

PER SERVING

Calories: 610 | Fat: 51g | Protein: 27g | Total Carbs: 15g | Net Carbs: 11g | Fiber: 4g | Sugar: 9g | Sodium: 1955mg | Macros: Fat: 72% | Protein: 19% | Carbs: 9%

Hemp Cobb Salad

Prep time: 10 minutes | Cook time:5 minutes |Serves 2

- 2 cups fresh spinach leaves
- 4 hardboiled eggs, chopped
- ¼ cup diced cucumber
- 1 avocado, sliced
- ¼ cup diced tomato
- 4 slices cooked vegan bacon, sliced
- 4 tablespoons hemp seeds
- 2 tablespoons diced scallions, white and green parts
- 4 tablespoons blue cheese
- 4 ounces blue cheese dressing

1. Divide the spinach leaves between two bowls.
2. Arrange half the eggs, cucumber, avocado, tomato, and bacon in sections on top of each bowl of spinach.
3. Sprinkle each salad with half the hemp seeds, scallions, and blue cheese.
4. Top each salad with the dressing and serve.

PER SERVING

Calories: 858 | Fat: 72g | Protein: 32g | Total Carbs: 20g | Net Carbs: 11g | Fiber: 9g | Sugar: 4g | Sodium: 1242mg | Macros: Fat: 76% | Protein: 15% | Carbs: 9%

Mediterranean Salad
Prep time: 10 minutes | Cook time:5 minutes |Serves 2

- 3 tablespoons olive oil
- 2 tablespoons red wine vinegar
- 3 garlic cloves, minced
- ½ teaspoon salt
- ¼ teaspoon freshly ground black pepper
- 1 head romaine lettuce, leaves torn into small pieces
- ½ red onion, sliced
- ½ cup diced cucumber
- 24 Kalamata olives
- 2 small Campari tomatoes, diced and seeded
- 1 cup crumbled feta cheese

1. In a small bowl, mix together the olive oil, vinegar, garlic, salt, and pepper. Set aside.
2. In a large bowl, combine the lettuce, onion, cucumber, olives, tomatoes, and feta cheese.
3. Pour the dressing over the salad and toss it well to coat the ingredients. Divide equally between two bowls and serve.

PER SERVING

Calories: 515 | Fat: 43g | Protein: 13g | Total Carbs: 19g | Net Carbs: 15g | Fiber: 4g | Sugar: 8g | Sodium: 1794mg | Macros: Fat: 75% | Protein: 10% | Carbs: 15%

Avocado And Asparagus Salad
Prep time: 15 minutes | Cook time:2 minutes |Serves 4

- ½ pound asparagus, trimmed and halved
- 4 cups red leaf lettuce
- 1 cup cherry tomatoes, halved
- 1 ripe avocado, sliced
- 1 cup sliced mozzarella
- ¼ cup fresh basil leaves
- ⅓ cup olive oil
- 1 teaspoon freshly squeezed lemon juice
- ½ teaspoon Dijon mustard
- Salt
- Freshly ground black pepper

1. Prepare an ice bath by filling a large bowl with cold water and plenty of ice.
2. Put a pot of water over medium-high heat and bring to a boil. Add the asparagus to the boiling water and cook for 1 to 2 minutes.
3. Immediately drain the asparagus and transfer it to the ice bath to stop the cooking process. Let cool for 5 minutes.
4. Drain the asparagus and pat it dry with paper towels.
5. Layer equal amounts of lettuce, asparagus, tomatoes, avocado, mozzarella, and basil leaves on four serving plates.
6. In a small bowl, combine the olive oil, lemon juice, and Dijon mustard and add salt and pepper as needed.
7. Pour the dressing evenly over the salads and serve.

PER SERVING

Calories: 346 | Fat: 30g | Protein: 10g | Total Carbs: 9g | Net Carbs: 4g | Fiber: 5g | Sugar: 3g | Sodium: 235mg | Macros: Fat: 78% | Protein: 12% | Carbs: 10%

Chinese Style Cauliflower Rice
Prep time: 5 minutes | Cook time: 15 minutes |Serves 3

- 1/2 pound fresh cauliflower
- 1 tablespoon sesame oil
- 1/2 cup leeks, chopped
- 1 garlic, pressed
- Sea salt and freshly ground black pepper, to taste
- 1/2 teaspoon Chinese five-spice powder
- 1 teaspoon oyster sauce
- 1/2 teaspoon light soy sauce
- 1 tablespoon Shaoxing wine
- 3 eggs

1. Pulse the cauliflower in a food processor until it resembles rice.
2. Heat the sesame oil in a pan over medium-high heat; sauté the leeks and garlic for 2 to 3 minutes. Add the prepared cauliflower rice to the pan, along with salt, black pepper, and Chinese five-spice powder.
3. Next, add oyster sauce, soy sauce, and wine. Let it cook, stirring occasionally, until the cauliflower is crisp-tender, about 5 minutes.
4. Then, add the eggs to the pan; stir until everything is well combined. Serve warm and enjoy!

PER SERVING

Calories: 131 | Fat: 8.9g | Carbs: 6.2g | Fiber: 1.8g | Protein: 7.2g

Spinach with Paprika and Cheese
Prep time: 5 minutes | Cook time: 10 minutes |Serves 4

- 1 tablespoon butter, room temperature
- 1 clove garlic, minced
- 10 ounces spinach
- 1/2 teaspoon garlic salt
- 1/4 teaspoon ground black pepper, or more to taste
- 1/2 teaspoon cayenne pepper
- 3 ounces cream cheese
- 1/2 cup double cream

1. Melt the butter in a saucepan that is preheated over medium heat. Once hot. Cook garlic for 30 seconds.
2. Now, add the spinach; cover the pan for 2 minutes to let the spinach wilt. Season with salt, black pepper, and cayenne pepper
3. Stir in cheese and cream; stir until the cheese melts. Serve immediately.

PER SERVING

Calories: 166 | Fat: 15.1g | Carbs: 5g | Fiber: 1.7g | Protein: 4.4g

Summer Mediterranean Salad

Prep time: 5 minutes | Cook time: 20 minutes | Serves 4

- 1/2 pound Roma tomatoes, sliced
- 1 Lebanese cucumber, sliced
- 1 cup arugula
- 1/2 teaspoon oregano
- 1/2 teaspoon basil
- Sea salt, to season
- 4 tablespoons extra-virgin olive oil
- 2 tablespoons fresh lemon juice
- 1/2 cup Kalamata olives, pitted and sliced
- 4 ounces feta cheese, cubed

1. Arrange the Roma tomatoes and zucchini slices on a roasting pan; spritz cooking oil over your vegetables.
2. Bake in the preheated oven at 355 degrees F for 6 to 7 minutes. Let them cool slightly, then, transfer to a salad bowl.
3. Add in the cucumber, arugula, herbs, and spices. Drizzle olive oil and lemon juice over your veggies; toss to combine well.
4. Top with Kalamata olives and feta cheese. Serve at room temperature and enjoy!

PER SERVING

Calories: 243 | Fat: 22.2g | Carbs: 6.8g | Protein: 6.5g | Fiber: 1.9g

German Fried Cabbage

Prep time: 5 minutes | Cook time: 20 minutes | Serves 3

- 4 ounces bacon, diced
- 1 medium-sized onion, chopped
- 2 cloves garlic, minced
- 1/2 teaspoon caraway seeds
- 1 bay laurel
- 1/2 teaspoon cayenne pepper
- 1 pound red cabbage, shredded
- 1/4 teaspoon ground black pepper, to season
- 1 cup beef bone broth

1. Heat up a nonstick skillet over a moderate flame. Cook the bacon for 3 to 4 minutes, stirring continuously; set aside.
2. In the same skillet, sauté the onion for 2 to 3 minutes or until it has softened. Now, sauté the garlic and caraway seeds for 30 seconds more or until aromatic.
3. Then, add in the remaining ingredients and stir to combine. Reduce the temperature to medium-low, cover, and cook for 10 minutes longer; stirring periodically to ensure even cooking.
4. Serve in individual bowls, garnished with the reserved bacon. Enjoy!

PER SERVING

Calories: 243 | Fat: 22.2g | Carbs: 6.8g | Protein: 6.5g | Fiber: 1.9g

Authentic Fennel Avgolemono

Prep time: 10 minutes | Cook time: 25 minutes | Serves 6

- 2 tablespoons olive oil
- 1 celery stalk, chopped
- 1 pound fennel bulbs, sliced
- 1 garlic clove, minced
- 1 bay laurel
- 1 thyme sprig
- 5 cups chicken stock
- Sea salt and ground black pepper, to season
- 2 eggs
- 1 tablespoon freshly squeezed lemon juice

1. Heat the olive oil in a heavy-bottomed pot over a medium-high flame. Now, sauté the celery and fennel until they have softened but not browned, about 8 minutes.
2. Add in the garlic, bay laurel, and thyme sprig; continue sautéing until aromatic an additional minute or so.
3. Add the chicken stock, salt, and black pepper to the pot. Bring to a boil. Reduce the heat to medium-low and let it simmer, partially covered, approximately 13 minutes.
4. Discard the bay laurel and then, blend your soup with an immersion blender.
5. Whisk the eggs and lemon juice; gradually pour 2 cups of the hot soup into the egg mixture, whisking constantly.
6. Return the soup to the pot and continue stirring for a few minutes or just until thickened. Serve warm.

PER SERVING

Calories: 86 | Fat: 6.1g | Carbs: 6g | Protein: 2.8g | Fiber: 2.4g

Broiled Avocado with Parmigiano Reggiano

Prep time: 5 minutes | Cook time: 15 minutes | Serves 6

- 3 avocados, pitted and halved
- 1/2 teaspoon red pepper flakes, crushed
- 1/2 teaspoon Himalayan salt
- 3 tablespoons extra-virgin olive oil
- 6 tablespoons Parmigiano-Reggiano cheese, grated

1. Begin by preheating your oven for broil.
2. Then, cut a crisscross pattern about 3/4 of the way through on each avocado half with a sharp knife.
3. Sprinkle red pepper and salt over the avocado halves. Drizzle olive oil over them and top with the grated Parmigiano-Reggiano cheese.
4. Transfer the avocado halves to a roasting pan and cook under the broiler approximately 5 minutes. Enjoy!

PER SERVING

Calories: 196 | Fat: 18.8g | Carbs: 6.5g | 2.7g Protein: | Fiber: 4.6g

Superb Mushroom Mélange

Prep time: 10 minutes | Cook time: 20 minutes |Serves 6

- 4 tablespoons olive oil
- 1 bell pepper, sliced
- 1/2 cup leeks, finely diced
- 2 cloves garlic, smashed
- 2 pounds brown mushrooms, sliced
- 2 cups chicken broth
- 1 cup tomato sauce
- 1/2 teaspoon dried oregano
- 1/2 teaspoon chili powder
- 1/2 teaspoon paprika
- 1/2 teaspoon ground black pepper
- Sea salt, to taste

1. Heat the oil in a heavy-bottomed pot over medium-high flame. Now, sauté bell pepper along with the leeks for about 5 minutes.
2. Stir in the garlic and mushrooms, and continue sautéing an additional minute or so. Add in a splash of chicken broth to deglaze the bottom of the pan.
3. After that, add in the tomato sauce and seasonings. Bring to a boil and immediately reduce the heat to simmer.
4. Partially cover and cook for 8 to 10 minutes more or until the mushrooms are cooked through.
5. Ladle into individual bowls and serve with cauli rice if desired. Bon appétit!

PER SERVING

Calories: 123 | Fat: 9.2g | Carbs: 5.8g | Protein: 4.7g | Fiber: 1.4g

Roasted Portobellos with Edam and Herbs

Prep time: 5 minutes | Cook time: 45 minutes |Serves 2

- 2 tablespoons ghee, melted
- 1 pound white portobello mushrooms, cleaned and sliced
- 1/4 teaspoon smoked paprika
- 1/2 teaspoon cayenne pepper
- 1/4 teaspoon black pepper, cracked
- 1/2 teaspoon dried oregano
- 1/2 teaspoon dried basil
- Sea salt, to taste
- 3 ounces edam cheese, shredded
- 1 tablespoon fresh cilantro, chopped
- 1/2 tablespoon fresh tarragon, chopped

1. Drizzle the melted ghee over your portobellos. Sprinkle the smoked paprika, cayenne pepper, black pepper, oregano, basil, and salt over your mushrooms.
2. Roast in the preheated oven at 370 degrees F for about 35 minutes or until they have softened; at the halfway point, turn them over to ensure even cooking.

3. Scatter the edam cheese over your mushrooms and roast an additional 4 to 5 minutes or until it is bubbling.
4. Serve warm, garnished with fresh cilantro and tarragon. Bon appétit!

PER SERVING

Calories: 308 | Fat: 24.1g | Carbs: 6.1g | Protein: 17.9g | Fiber: 2.8g

Zoodles with Romano Cheese and Mushroom Sauce

Prep time: 5 minutes | Cook time: 15 minutes |Serves 3

- 1 ½ tablespoons olive oil
- 3 cups button mushrooms, chopped
- 2 cloves garlic, smashed
- 1 cup tomato puree
- 1 pound zucchini, spiralized
- Salt and ground black pepper, to taste
- 1/3 cup Pecorino Romano cheese, preferably freshly grated

1. Heat the olive oil in a saucepan over a moderate flame. Then, cook the mushrooms until tender and fragrant or about 4 minutes.
2. Stir in the garlic and continue to sauté an additional 30 seconds or until just tender and aromatic. Fold in the tomato puree and zucchini.
3. Reduce the heat to medium-low, partially cover and let it cook for about 6 minutes or until heated through. Season with salt and black pepper to taste.
4. Divide your zoodles and sauce between serving plates. Top with Pecorino Romano cheese and serve warm. Bon appétit!

PER SERVING

Calories: 160 | Fat: 10.6g | Carbs: 7.4g | Protein: 10g | Fiber: 3.4g

Italian Style Baked Eggplant Rounds

Prep time: 5 minutes | Cook time: 40 minutes |Serves 6

- 1 pound eggplant, peeled and sliced
- 2 teaspoons Italian seasoning blend
- 1/2 teaspoon cayenne pepper
- 1/2 teaspoon salt
- 1½ cups marinara sauce
- 1 cup mozzarella cheese
- 2 tablespoons fresh basil leaves, snipped

1. Begin by preheating your oven to 380 degrees F. Line a baking pan with parchment paper.
2. Now, arrange the eggplant rounds on the baking pan. Season with the Italian blend, cayenne pepper, and salt.
3. Bake for 25 to 28 minutes, flipping the rounds half-way through baking time.
4. Next, remove from the oven and top with the marinara sauce and mozzarella cheese.
5. Bake for 6 to 8 minutes more until mozzarella is bubbling. Garnish with fresh basil leaves just before serving.

PER SERVING

Calories: 91 | Fat: 4.8g | Carbs: 5.3g | Protein: 5.3g | Fiber: 2.9g

Peasant Stir Fry (Satarash)

Prep time: 5 minutes | Cook time: 25 minutes |Serves 5

- 2 tablespoons olive oil
- 1 yellow onion, sliced
- 3 garlic cloves, halved
- 8 bell peppers, deveined and cut into strips
- 1 tomato, chopped
- 1/2 teaspoon ground black pepper
- 1/2 teaspoon paprika
- 1/2 teaspoon kosher salt
- 2 eggs

1. Heat the olive oil in a frying pan over medium-low heat. Now, sweat the onion for 3 to 4 minutes or until tender.
2. Now, stir in the garlic and peppers; continue sautéing for 5 minutes. Then, add in the tomato, black pepper, paprika, and kosher salt.
3. Partially cover and continue to cook for a further 6 to 8 minutes.
4. Fold in the eggs and stir fry for another 5 minutes. Serve warm and enjoy!

PER SERVING

Calories: 114 | Fat: 7.6g | Carbs: 6g | Protein: 3.4g | Fiber: 1.5g

Cream of Broccoli Cheese Soup

Prep time: 5 minutes | Cook time: 25 minutes |Serves 4

- 3 tablespoons olive oil
- 1 celery rib, chopped
- 1/2 white onion, finely chopped
- 1 teaspoon ginger-garlic paste
- 1 (1-pound) head broccoli, broken into florets
- 4 cups vegetable broth
- 1/2 cup double cream
- 1½ cups Monterey Jack cheese, grated

1. Heat the olive oil in a soup pot over moderate heat. Now, sauté the celery rib and onion until they have softened.
2. Fold in the ginger-garlic paste and broccoli; pour in the vegetable broth and bring to boil. Turn the heat to simmer. Continue to cook for a further 13 minutes or until the broccoli is cooked through.
3. Fold in the cream, stir and remove from heat. Divide your soup between four ramekins and top them with the Monterey Jack cheese.
4. Broil for about 5 minutes or until cheese is bubbly and golden. Bon appétit!

PER SERVING

Calories: 323 | Fat: 28.2g | Carbs: 4.4g | Protein: 13.4g | Fiber: 0.6g

Loaded Keto Coleslaw

Prep time: 5 minutes | Cook time: 10 minutes |Serves 4

- 2 teaspoons balsamic vinegar
- 1 teaspoon fresh garlic, minced
- 2 tablespoons tahini (sesame paste)
- 1 tablespoon yellow mustard
- Sea salt and ground black pepper, to taste
- 1/4 teaspoon paprika
- 1 red bell pepper, deveined and sliced
- 1 green bell pepper, deveined and sliced
- 1/2 pound Napa cabbage, shredded
- 2 cups arugula, torn into pieces
- 1 Spanish onion, thinly sliced into rings
- 4 tablespoons sesame seeds, lightly toasted

1. Make a dressing by whisking the balsamic vinegar, garlic, tahini, mustard, salt, black pepper, and paprika.
2. In a salad bowl, combine the bell peppers, cabbage, arugula, and Spanish onion. Dress the salad and toss until everything is well incorporated.
3. Garnish with sesame seeds just before serving. Serve well chilled and enjoy!

PER SERVING

Calories: 122 | Fat: 9.1g | Carbs: 5.9g | Protein: 4.5g | Fiber: 3g

Hearty Chanterelle Stew with Za'atar Oil

Prep time: 5 minutes | Cook time: 1 hour 50 minutes | Serves 4

- 1/2 teaspoon Za'atar spice
- 4 tablespoons olive oil
- 1/2 cup shallots, chopped
- 2 bell peppers, chopped
- 1 poblano pepper, finely chopped
- 8 ounces Chanterelle mushroom, sliced
- 1/2 teaspoon garlic, minced
- Sea salt and freshly cracked black pepper, to taste
- 1 cup tomato puree
- 3 cups vegetable broth
- 1 bay laurel

1. Combine the Za'atar with 3 tablespoons of olive oil in a small saucepan. Cook over a moderate flame until hot; make sure not to burn the zaatar. Set aside for 1 hour to cool and infuse.
2. In a heavy-bottomed pot, heat the remaining tablespoon of olive oil. Now, sauté the shallots and bell peppers until just tender and fragrant.
3. Stir in the poblano pepper, mushrooms, and garlic; continue to sauté until the mushrooms have softened.
4. Next, add in the salt, black pepper, tomato puree, broth, and bay laurel. Once your stew begins to boil, turn the heat down to a simmer.
5. Let it simmer for about 40 minutes until everything is thoroughly cooked. Ladle into individual bowls and drizzle each serving with Za'atar oil. Bon appétit!

PER SERVING
Calories: 155 | Fat: 13.9g | Carbs: 6g | Protein: 1.4g | Fiber: 2.9g

Traditional Provençal Ratatouille with Eggs

Prep time: 10 minutes | Cook time: 35 minutes | Serves 6

- 2 tablespoons olive oil
- 2 garlic cloves, finely minced
- 1 red pepper, sliced
- 1 yellow pepper, sliced
- 1 green pepper, sliced
- 1 shallot, sliced
- 1 large-sized zucchini, sliced
- 3 tomatoes, sliced
- 1 cup vegetable broth
- Sea salt, to taste
- 1/2 teaspoon dried oregano
- 1/2 teaspoon dried parsley flakes
- 1/2 teaspoon paprika
- 1/2 teaspoon ground black pepper
- 6 eggs

1. Start by preheating your oven to 400 degrees F. Brush the sides and bottom of a baking pan with olive oil.
2. Layer all vegetables into the prepared pan and cover tightly with foil. Pour in the vegetable broth. Season with salt, oregano, parsley, paprika, and ground black pepper.
3. Bake for about 25 minutes.
4. Create six indentations in the hot ratatouille. Break an egg into each indentation. Bake until the eggs are set or about 9 minutes. Enjoy!

PER SERVING
Calories: 439 | Fat: 45g | Carbs: 5.5g | Protein: 6.5g | Fiber: 1g

Chapter 10
Desserts & Drinks

Chocolate Cake with Cream Cheese Frosting

Prep time: 10 minutes | Cook time: 25 minutes |Serves 10

- 1 stick butter, room temperature
- 1/3 cup full-fat milk
- 2 eggs
- 1/2 cup walnut meal
- 1/3 cup flaxseed meal
- 1/3 cup coconut flour
- 2 teaspoon baking powder
- 2 teaspoons liquid stevia
- 1/4 teaspoon ground star anise
- 1/4 teaspoon cinnamon
- 1/4 teaspoon ground cloves
- A pinch of flaky salt
- 2 tablespoons cocoa powder
- 1 teaspoon rum extract
- 1/3 cup butter, room temperature
- 6 ounces cream cheese, softened
- 1/2 cup Xylitol
- 1/2 teaspoon pure caramel extract

1. Cream the butter and milk with an electric mixer; slowly, fold in the eggs and beat again to combine well.
2. In another bowl, mix all types of flours with the baking powder, stevia, spices, cocoa powder, and rum extract.
3. Now, stir this dry mixture into the wet mixture; mix again until everything is well incorporated.
4. Press the batter into a parchment-lined baking pan. Bake in the preheated oven at 395 degrees F for 18 minutes.
5. Meanwhile, whip the butter and cream cheese with an electric mixer.
6. Add in the Xylitol and caramel extract; continue to beat until the sweetener is well dissolved and the frosting is creamy.
7. Frost your cake and serve well-chilled. Bon appétit!

PER SERVING

Calories: 292 | Fat: 29.1g | Carbs: 5.5g | Protein: 5.3g | Fiber: 2.4g

Chewy Chocolate Chip Cookies

Prep time: 10 minutes | Cook time: 20 minutes |Serves 1

- 1½ cups blanched almond flour
- ½ cup granular erythritol
- 1 tablespoon unflavored beef gelatin powder
- 1 teaspoon baking powder
- ½ cup (1 stick) unsalted butter, melted but not hot
- 1 large egg
- 1 teaspoon vanilla extract
- ½ cup sugar-free chocolate chips

1. Preheat the oven to 350°F and line 2 baking sheets with parchment paper.

2. Put the almond flour, erythritol, gelatin, and baking powder in a medium-sized bowl and whisk using a fork. Set aside.
3. Put the melted butter, egg, and vanilla extract in a large bowl and combine using a hand mixer or whisk. Add the dry mixture to wet mixture in 2 batches and combine until you have a soft dough that can easily be rolled between your hands without sticking.
4. Fold the chocolate chips into the dough with a rubber spatula. Using a cookie scoop or spoon, scoop 16 even-sized balls of the dough onto the baking sheets, leaving 2 inches of space between them. Using your hand or the spatula, flatten the cookies a little. They will spread slightly in the oven.
5. Bake for 20 minutes, or until golden brown. Allow to cool on the baking sheets for 15 minutes prior to handling.
6. Store leftovers in a sealed container in the refrigerator for up to a week or freeze for up to a month.

PER SERVING

Calories: 125 | Fat: 11.8 g | Protein: 2.8 g | Carbs: 3.2g | Fiber: 1.5 g | Sugar Alcohol: 6.6 g

Pistachio Coconut Fudge

Prep time: 10 minutes | Cook time: 5 minutes |Serves 1

- ½ cup coconut oil, melted
- 4 ounces cream cheese (½ cup), room temperature
- 1 teaspoon vanilla extract
- ¼ teaspoon plus 10 drops of liquid stevia
- ½ cup shelled raw pistachios, roughly chopped, divided
- ½ cup unsweetened shredded coconut, divided

1. In a medium-sized bowl, beat the coconut oil and cream cheese with a hand mixer until smooth and creamy. Add the vanilla extract and stevia and mix until combined.
2. Fold in one-third of the pistachios and one-third of the coconut flakes using a rubber spatula. Pour the fudge mixture into a 5-inch square dish or pan and top with the remaining pistachios and shredded coconut.
3. Refrigerate for at least 2 hours prior to serving. To serve, cut into 16 pieces.
4. Store leftovers in a sealed container in the refrigerator for up to a week.

PER SERVING

Calories: 123 | Fat: 12.9 g | Protein: 1.2 G Carbs 2g | Fiber: 0.7 g

Extreme Fudge Brownies

Prep time: 10 minutes | Cook time: 52 minutes |Serves 1

- ¼ cup cocoa powder
- 2 tablespoons coconut flour
- ¼ teaspoon pink Himalayan salt
- 3 large eggs
- ½ cup granular erythritol
- ½ teaspoon vanilla extract
- ¾ cup (1½ sticks) unsalted butter
- 2 ounces unsweetened baking chocolate (100% cacao)
- Powdered erythritol, for topping (optional)

1. Preheat the oven to 325°F and grease an 8-inch square brownie pan with coconut oil spray.
2. Put the cocoa powder, coconut flour, and salt in a small bowl and whisk using a fork. Set aside.
3. In a large bowl, whisk together the eggs, erythritol, and vanilla extract. Set aside.
4. In a small microwave-safe bowl, combine the butter and chocolate. Microwave until fully melted, about 1 minute, stirring every 30 seconds. Add the melted chocolate mixture to the egg mixture and whisk to combine.
5. Add the dry mixture to the wet mixture in 2 batches, whisking after each addition until fully combined.
6. Pour the batter into the greased pan and bake for 50 minutes, or until a toothpick inserted in the center comes out clean. Allow to cool in the pan for 20 minutes, then cut into 9 pieces. If desired, dust with powdered erythritol before serving.
7. Store leftovers in a sealed container in the refrigerator for up to a week or freeze for up to a month.

PER SERVING

Calories: 210 | Fat: 19.9 g | Protein: 3.7 g | Carbs: 4.1g | Fiber: 2.8 g | Sugar Alcohol: 10.7 g

Peanut Butter Hemp Heart Cookies

Prep time: 10 minutes | Cook time: 14 minutes |Serves 1

- ½ cup natural peanut butter, room temperature
- 1 large egg
- ½ cup hemp hearts
- ¼ cup granular erythritol
- ¼ teaspoon baking powder
- ½ teaspoon vanilla extract
- ½ cup sugar-free chocolate chips

1. Preheat the oven to 350°F and line 2 baking sheets with parchment paper.
2. In a large mixing bowl, combine the peanut butter and egg using a whisk. Add the hemp hearts, erythritol, baking powder, and vanilla extract and combine using a wooden spoon. Fold in the chocolate chips.
3. Using a cookie scoop or spoon, scoop 12 even-sized balls of the dough onto the lined baking sheets, spacing them about 2 inches apart.

Flatten the cookies with a fork.

4. Bake the cookies for 12 to 14 minutes, until golden brown and slightly firm to touch. Allow to cool on the baking sheets for 10 minutes prior to handling or they will fall apart.
5. Store leftovers in a sealed container in the refrigerator for up to a week or freeze for up to a month.

PER SERVING

Calories: 120 | Fat: 9.8 g | Protein: 5.7 g | Carbs: 4.1g | Fiber: 2.2 g | Sugar Alcohol: 4.8 g

Vanilla Egg Custard

Prep time: 10 minutes | Cook time: 30 minutes |Serves 2

- 1 cup heavy whipping cream, plus ¼ cup for topping if desired
- 2 large egg yolks
- 2 teaspoons vanilla extract
- ½ teaspoon liquid stevia

1. Preheat the oven to 300°F.
2. Put the 1 cup of cream, egg yolks, vanilla extract, and stevia in a medium-sized mixing bowl and beat with a hand mixer until combined. Pour into two 6-ounce ramekins. Place the ramekins in a baking dish and fill the baking dish with boiling water so that it goes two-thirds of the way up the sides of the ramekins.
3. Bake for 30 minutes, or until the edges of the custard are just starting to brown. It should not be completely baked through and firm. Place in the refrigerator to chill and set for at least 2 hours before serving.
4. If making the topping, put the ¼ cup of cream in a medium-sized mixing bowl and whip using the hand mixer until soft peaks form. Top the custard with the whipped cream prior to serving.

PER SERVING

Calories: 568 | Fat: 59.5 g | Protein: 5.5 g | Carbs: 4.5g | Fiber: 0 g

Instant Protein Ice Cream

Prep time: 1 minutes | Cook time: 5 minutes |Serves 1

- 1 cup unsweetened almond milk
- 1 scoop flavored protein powder of choice
- ¼ teaspoon xanthan gum
- 1½ cups ice
- Ground cinnamon, for garnish (optional)

1. Put the milk in a blender. Add the protein powder, xanthan gum, and ice and puree on high until the mixture is smooth, 20 to 30 seconds.
2. Pour into a serving bowl and garnish with a dusting of cinnamon, if desired. Enjoy immediately.

PER SERVING

Calories: 130 | Fat: 5 g | Protein: 21 g | Carbs: 5g | Fiber: 2 g

Strawberry Shortcakes

Prep time: 20 minutes | Cook time: 20 minutes | Serves 6

SHORTCAKES:

- ¼ cup plus 2 tablespoons coconut flour
- 1 packet sugar-free strawberry-flavored gelatin powder
- 1 teaspoon baking powder
- ¼ teaspoon pink Himalayan salt
- ¼ cup plus 2 tablespoons coconut oil, melted
- 2 ounces cream cheese (¼ cup), room temperature
- ¼ cup sour cream
- 4 large eggs, room temperature
- 15 drops of liquid stevia

FILLING/TOPPING:

- 1 cup heavy whipping cream
- 1 cup fresh strawberries, hulled and thinly sliced
- Special Equipment:
- 6-cavity, 3½-inch-diameter silicone muffin top pan

1. Preheat the oven to 350°F and grease a 6-cavity silicone muffin top pan with coconut oil spray.
2. Make the shortcakes: In a small bowl, whisk together the coconut flour, gelatin, baking powder, and salt.
3. Put the coconut oil, cream cheese, and sour cream in a large mixing bowl and combine with the whisk. Add the eggs and stevia and whisk until smooth.
4. Add the dry mixture to the wet ingredients and whisk until fully incorporated and smooth. Evenly distribute the mixture among the greased cavities of the muffin top pan, filling them to the rim. Level the tops with a butter knife.
5. Bake for 20 minutes, or until a toothpick inserted in the center of a cake comes out clean. Allow to cool in the pan for 5 minutes, then transfer the shortcakes to a cooling rack to cool completely before filling.
6. Make the filling/topping: Put the cream in a medium-sized mixing bowl and beat using a hand mixer until stiff peaks form.
7. Assemble the shortcakes: Slice the cakes in half horizontally to create a total of 12 round layers. Using a butter knife, frost the bottom halves with the whipped cream, then make a single layer of overlapping strawberries. Put the other half of each cake on top of the strawberries and frost the tops using a piping bag or butter knife. Make a top layer of sliced strawberries. (We like to fan the berry slices for a pretty presentation.)
8. Store leftovers in a sealed container in the refrigerator for up to a week.

PER SERVING

Calories: 392 | Fat: 36.8 g | Protein: 6.2 g | Carbs: 8.6g | Fiber: 3 g

Chia Protein Smoothie Bowl

Prep time: 5 minutes | Cook time: 5 minutes | Serves 2

- 2 tablespoons chia seeds
- 4 tablespoons peanut butter
- 1/2 cup coconut milk
- 4 tablespoons powdered erythritol
- A pinch of freshly grated nutmeg

1. Process all ingredients in your blender until well combined.
2. Pour into serving bowls and serve well-chilled. Enjoy!

PER SERVING

Calories: 280 | Fat: 16g | Carbs: 7g | Protein: 25g | Fiber: 4g

Keto Whipped Cream

Prep time: 5 minutes | Cook time: 5 minutes | Serves 6

- ⅔ cup heavy whipping cream
- 1 tablespoon plus 1 teaspoon Swerve confectioners'-style sweetener
- 1 teaspoon vanilla extract

1. Place all the ingredients in a medium-sized mixing bowl and blend with a hand mixer until stiff peaks form, 3 to 4 minutes.

PER SERVING

Calories: 89.6 | Fat: 8.8 g | Protein: 0 g | Total Carbs: 3.8 g | Net Carbs: 1.8 g

Puffy Anise Cookies

Prep time: 5 minutes | Cook time: 25 minutes | Serves 10

- 2 tablespoons coconut oil
- 1 tablespoon coconut milk
- 1 egg, whisked
- 1 cup coconut flour
- 1 cup almond flour
- 1 teaspoon pure anise extract
- 1/4 teaspoon ground cloves
- 1/2 teaspoon ground cinnamon
- A pinch of salt

1. In a mixing bowl, beat the coconut oil, coconut milk, and egg. In a separate bowl, mix the flour, baking powder, monk fruit, anise extract, ground cloves, cinnamon, and salt.
2. Add the dry mixture to the wet mixture; mix to combine well. Shape the mixture into small balls and arrange them on a parchment-lined baking pan.
3. Bake at 360 degrees F for 13 minutes. Transfer to cooling racks for 10 minutes. Bon appétit!

PER SERVING

Calories: 142 | Fat: 13g | Carbs: 5.2g | Protein: 3.5g | Fiber: 2.4g

Caramel Chocolate Pudding

Prep time: 5 minutes | Cook time: 1 hour 10 minutes |Serves 3

- 2 ounces cream cheese, at room temperature
- 1/2 cup double cream
- 1 teaspoon caramel extract
- 4 tablespoons cocoa powder, unsweetened
- 1/2 cup Swerve
- A pinch of salt
- A pinch of grated nutmeg

1. In a large bowl, whip the cream cheese and double cream until firm peaks form.
2. Fold in the caramel extract, cocoa powder, Swerve, salt, and nutmeg. Blend until well mixed.
3. Cover the bowl with a lid and refrigerate at least 1 hour. Bon appétit!

PER SERVING

Calories: 154 | Fat: 14.8g | Carbs: 6g | Protein: 2.8g | Fiber: 2.4g

Chocolate Almond Squares

Prep time: 5 minutes | Cook time: 55 minutes |Serves 10

- 1/2 cup coconut flour 1/2 cup almond meal
- 1 cup almond butter
- 1/4 cup erythritol
- 2 tablespoons coconut oil
- 1/2 cup sugar-free bakers' chocolate, chopped into small chunks

1. Mix the coconut flour, almond meal, butter, and erythritol until smooth.
2. Press the mixture into a parchment-lined square pan. Place in your freezer for 30 minutes.
3. Meanwhile, microwave the coconut oil and bakers' chocolate for 40 seconds. Pour the glaze over the cake and transfer to your freezer until the chocolate is set or about 20 minutes.
4. Cut into squares and enjoy!

PER SERVING

Calories: 234 | Fat: 25.1g | Carbs: 3.6g | Protein: 1.7g | Fiber: 1.4g

No Bake Energy Bites

Prep time: 5 minutes | Cook time: 10 minutes |Serves 10

- 1/2 cup coconut flour
- 1/2 cup almond meal
- 1/4 cup erythritol
- 2 tablespoons milk
- 1/2 cup peanut butter, melted
- 1/4 teaspoon ground cinnamon
- 1/4 teaspoon ground star anise
- 1 teaspoon vanilla paste
- 1/8 teaspoon coarse sea salt
- 1/4 cup chocolate chips, sugar-free

1. Mix the coconut flour, almond meal, erythritol, milk, peanut butter, cinnamon, anise vanilla, and salt until everything is well incorporated and smooth.
2. Now, fold in the chocolate chips and gently stir to combine well.
3. Spoon the mixture into ice-cube molds.
4. Place in your refrigerator for 1 hour before serving and unmolding. Bon appétit!

PER SERVING

Calories: 102 | Fat: 7.8g | Carbs: 5.8g | Protein: 2.6g | Fiber: 1.8g

Blueberry Pudding Bowl

Prep time: 5 minutes | Cook time: 10 minutes |Serves 1

- 1/3 avocado, pitted and peeled
- 1/4 cup frozen cauliflower rice
- 2 tablespoons blueberries
- 2 tablespoons Greek-style yogurt
- 1 tablespoon Swerve
- 1/4 teaspoon pure vanilla essence
- 1 tablespoon peanut butter
- 1 tablespoon chia seeds

1. Process the avocado, cauliflower rice, blueberries, yogurt, Swerve, and vanilla in your blender until creamy and smooth.
2. Spoon into a serving bowl; top with the peanut butter and chia seeds. Devour!

PER SERVING

Calories: 136 | Fat: 10.5g | Carbs: 6.9g | Protein: 3.1g | Fiber: 5g

Greek Style Cheesecake

Prep time: 10 minutes | Cook time: 2 hours 20 minutes | Serves 10

- 1/2 cup coconut flour
- 1/2 cup almond flour
- 2 tablespoons pecans, ground
- 2 tablespoons golden flaxseed meal
- 6 tablespoons xylitol
- 1/2 teaspoon cinnamon
- 1 ounce Greek-style yogurt
- 36 ounces cream cheese, room temperature
- 4 eggs
- 1½ cups xylitol
- 1/2 teaspoons almond extract
- 1/2 teaspoons vanilla extract

1. In a mixing bowl, thoroughly combine all the ingredients for the crust. Press the mixture into a lightly greased baking pan. Place in your refrigerator for 30 minutes.
2. In the meantime, beat the Greek-style yogurt with the cream cheese until smooth and fluffy. Then, fold in the eggs, xylitol, almond, and vanilla extract; beat on medium speed until well combined.
3. Spread the filling on the crust using a rubber spatula. Add 1-inch of hot water to a large roasting pan for the water bath.
4. Place the baking pan inside of the roasting pan.
5. Bake in the preheated oven for about 60 minutes until the center is almost set.
6. Heat off; open the oven door slightly. Let it sit in the oven in the water bath for about 50 minutes. After that, cool your cheesecake completely at room temperature.
7. Afterwards, refrigerate your cheesecake for at least 4 hours. Enjoy!

PER SERVING

Calories: 483 | Fat: 47.2g | Carbs: 5.8g | Protein: 10.3g | Fiber: 1.7g

Morning Coffee

Prep time: 5 minutes | Cook time: 45 minutes | Serves 9

- 1½ cups brewed coffee, hot
- 2 tablespoons heavy whipping cream
- 1 tablespoon MCT oil
- 1 or 2 drops vanilla extract (optional)
- Stevia or other keto-friendly sweetener of choice, to taste (optional)

1. Pour the hot coffee into a mug. Add the cream, MCT oil, vanilla (if using), and sweetener (if using).
2. Stir well with a spoon or, for a frothier drink, use a milk frother.
3. Serve.

PER SERVING

Calories: 202 | Fat: 24 g | Protein: 0 g | Total Carbs: 2 g | Net Carbs: 2 g

Cheesecake Fat Bombs

Prep time: 5 minutes | Cook time: 35 minutes | Serves 6

- 6 ounces cream cheese
- 1/2 cup peanut butter
- 1/2 cup coconut butter
- 1/3 cup cocoa powder, unsweetened
- 2 tablespoons butter
- 1/2 teaspoon vanilla extract
- 1/4 teaspoon ground cinnamon
- 4 tablespoons confectioners' Swerve

1. In a mixing bowl, whisk all the ingredients until smooth and there are no lumps.
2. Pour the mixture into candy molds and transfer to your freezer until relatively hard on top or about 30 minutes.
3. Serve well chilled. Devour!

PER SERVING

Calories: 406 | Fat: 40.5g | Carbs: 6.7g | Protein: 7.5g | Fiber: 2.5g

Keto Hot Chocolate

Prep time: 2 minutes | Cook time: 3 minutes | Serves 1

- 1 cup unsweetened almond milk
- 2 tablespoons heavy whipping cream
- 2 tablespoons Swerve confectioners'-style sweetener
- 1 tablespoon unsweetened cocoa powder, plus extra for dusting (optional) Keto Whipped Cream , for serving (optional)

1. In a small saucepan over medium heat, combine all the ingredients.
2. Whisk well for 2 to 3 minutes or until the desired temperature is reached.
3. Serve topped with whipped cream and a dusting of cocoa powder, if desired.

PER SERVING

Calories: 142 | Fat: 14 g | Protein: 2 g | Total Carbs: 24 g | Net Carbs: 3 g

Basic Orange Cheesecake

Prep time: 5 minutes | Cook time:15 minutes |Serves 12

- 1 tablespoon Swerve
- 1 cup almond flour
- 1 stick butter, room temperature 1/2 cup unsweetened coconut, shredded

FILLING:

- 1 teaspoon powdered gelatin
- 2 tablespoons Swerve
- 17 ounces mascarpone cream
- 2 tablespoon orange juice

1. Thoroughly combine all the ingredients for the crust; press the crust mixture into a lightly greased baking dish.
2. Let it stand in your refrigerator.
3. Then, mix 1 cup of boiling water and gelatin until all dissolved. Pour in 1 cup of cold water.
4. Add Swerve, mascarpone cheese, and orange juice; blend until smooth and uniform. Pour the filling onto the prepared crust. Enjoy!

PER SERVING

Calories: 150 | Fat: 15.4g | Carbs: 2.1g | Fiber: 0.1g |Protein: 1.2g

Mint, Cucumber, And Lime Infused Water

Prep time: 5 minutes | Cook time:10 minutes |Serves 2

- 2 quarts water
- 1 cup sliced cucumbers
- 10 to 12 fresh mint leaves, muddled
- 1 lime, thinly sliced
- Fresh mint sprigs, for garnish (optional)

1. Place all the ingredients in a pitcher and allow to infuse for at least 1hour before drinking. Serve with fresh mint sprigs, if desired.
2. Store in an airtight container (such as a mason jar, water bottle, or jug) in the refrigerator for up to a week.

PER SERVING

Calories: 0 | Fat: 0 g | Protein: 0 g | Total Carbs: 0 g | Net Carbs: 0 g

Peanut Butter and Chocolate Treat

Prep time: 5 minutes | Cook time:10 minutes | Serves 10

- 1 stick butter, room temperature
- 1/3 cup peanut butter
- 1/3 cup unsweetened cocoa powder
- 1/3 cup Swerve
- 1/2 teaspoon ground cinnamon
- A pinch of grated nutmeg
- 1/4 cup unsweetened coconut flakes
- 1/4 cup pork rinds, crushed

1. Melt the butter and peanut butter until smooth and uniform.
2. Add the remaining ingredients and mix until everything is well combined.
3. Line a baking sheet with a silicone baking mat. Pour the mixture into the baking sheet. Place in your freezer for 1 hour until ready to serve. Enjoy!

PER SERVING

Calories: 122 | Fat: 11.7g | Carbs: 4.9g | Fiber: 1.4g | Protein: 1.5g

Vanilla Mug Cake

Prep time: 5 minutes | Cook time:10 minutes |Serves 2

- 4 tablespoons psyllium husk flour
- 2 tablespoons ground flax seed
- 5 tablespoons almond flour
- 4 tablespoons Monk fruit powder
- A pinch of salt
- A pinch of grated nutmeg
- 1 teaspoon baking soda
- 4 tablespoons full-fat milk
- 1 teaspoon vanilla paste

1. Thoroughly combine all of the above ingredients in lightly greased mugs.
2. Then, microwave your cakes for 1 minute. Bon appétit!

PER SERVING

Calories: 143 | Fat: 10.7g | Carbs: 5.7g | Fiber: 2.6g | Protein: 5.7g

Classic Chocolate Mousse

Prep time: 5 minutes | Cook time: 5 minutes | Serves 2

- 4 tablespoons unsweetened cocoa powder
- 1/4 teaspoon vanilla essence
- 1/4 teaspoon rum extract
- 1/8 teaspoon ground cardamom
- 1/8 teaspoon grated nutmeg
- 4 tablespoons almond milk
- 2 ounces cream cheese
- 1/2 ripe avocado, pitted and peeled
- 1/4 cup swerve sweetener

1. Simply throw all ingredients into the bowl of your blender or a food processor.
2. Blend until everything is creamy and well incorporated.
3. Spoon into two dessert bowls. Serve well chilled. Bon appétit!

PER SERVING

Calories: 163 | Fat: 14.6g | Carbs: 9.8g | Protein: 4.7g | Fiber: 5.9g

Pecan Pie Chocolate Truffles

Prep time: 5 minutes | Cook time: 10 minutes | Serves 2

- 2 tablespoons coconut oil
- 1/4 cup coconut butter A pinch of salt
- A pinch of grated nutmeg
- 1/4 teaspoon ground cinnamon
- 3 tablespoons cocoa powder
- 1 teaspoon liquid Stevia
- 1/4 cup pecans, ground

1. In a mixing bowl, thoroughly combine all ingredients until everything is well blended and incorporated.
2. Scrape the batter into candy molds and keep in your freezer. Bon appétit!

PER SERVING

Calories: 436 | Fat: 47.6g | Carbs: 6.9g | Protein: 3.4g | Fiber: 4.5g

Strawberry Cream Ice Pops

Prep time: 5 minutes | Cook time:5 minutes | Serves 6

- 8 fresh strawberries, hulled and quartered
- 1 cup heavy whipping cream
- ½ cup unsweetened almond milk
- 2 ounces cream cheese, softened
- 2 ½ tablespoons Swerve confectioners'-style sweetener
- ½ teaspoon vanilla extract
- Special Equipment
- 6 standard-size ice pop molds

1. Place the strawberries and cream in a blender and blend until the cream starts to form peaks.
2. Add the almond milk, cream cheese, sweetener, and vanilla and blend until smooth. Pour into ice pop molds and freeze for at least 3 hours.
3. To remove the ice pops from the molds, run the molds under hot water. Store extras in the freezer for up to 3 weeks.

PER SERVING

Calories: 175 | Fat: 16.5 g | Protein: 1 g | Total Carbs: 8 g | Net Carbs: 3.8 g

Raspberry Cheesecake Fat Bombs

Prep time: 10 minutes | Cook time:45 minutes | Serves 3

- 12 fresh raspberries
- 6 ounces cream cheese, softened
- ¼ cup MCT oil
- 2 tablespoons unsalted butter
- ½ teaspoon vanilla extract
- 3 tablespoons Swerve confectioners'-style sweetener
- Special Equipment
- Silicone truffle mold(s) with at least 30 cavities (optional)

1. In a large mixing bowl, combine all the ingredients and mix with a fork until smooth.
2. Distribute the cheesecake mixture evenly among 30 cavities of a truffle mold(s). (Alternatively, use a spoon to dollop bite-sized portions of the mixture onto a sheet of parchment paper.) Freeze for 45 minutes or until set.
3. Store extras in the freezer for up to 3 weeks.

PER SERVING

Calories: 122 | Fat: 13.3 g | Protein: 1.2 g | Total Carbs: 0.9 g | Net Carbs: 0.8 g

Appendix 1 Measurement Conversion Chart

Volume Equivalents (Dry)

US STANDARD	METRIC (APPROXIMATE)
1/8 teaspoon	0.5 mL
1/4 teaspoon	1 mL
1/2 teaspoon	2 mL
3/4 teaspoon	4 mL
1 teaspoon	5 mL
1 tablespoon	15 mL
1/4 cup	59 mL
1/2 cup	118 mL
3/4 cup	177 mL
1 cup	235 mL
2 cups	475 mL
3 cups	700 mL
4 cups	1 L

Weight Equivalents

US STANDARD	METRIC (APPROXIMATE)
1 ounce	28 g
2 ounces	57 g
5 ounces	142 g
10 ounces	284 g
15 ounces	425 g
16 ounces (1 pound)	455 g
1.5 pounds	680 g
2 pounds	907 g

Volume Equivalents (Liquid)

US STANDARD	US STANDARD (OUNCES)	METRIC (APPROXIMATE)
2 tablespoons	1 fl.oz.	30 mL
1/4 cup	2 fl.oz.	60 mL
1/2 cup	4 fl.oz.	120 mL
1 cup	8 fl.oz.	240 mL
1 1/2 cup	12 fl.oz.	355 mL
2 cups or 1 pint	16 fl.oz.	475 mL
4 cups or 1 quart	32 fl.oz.	1 L
1 gallon	128 fl.oz.	4 L

Temperatures Equivalents

FAHRENHEIT(F)	CELSIUS(C) APPROXIMATE)
225 °F	107 °C
250 °F	120 ° °C
275 °F	135 °C
300 °F	150 °C
325 °F	160 °C
350 °F	180 °C
375 °F	190 °C
400 °F	205 °C
425 °F	220 °C
450 °F	235 °C
475 °F	245 °C
500 °F	260 °C

Appendix 2 The Dirty Dozen and Clean Fifteen

The Environmental Working Group (EWG) is a nonprofit, nonpartisan organization dedicated to protecting human health and the environment Its mission is to empower people to live healthier lives in a healthier environment. This organization publishes an annual list of the twelve kinds of produce, in sequence, that have the highest amount of pesticide residue-the Dirty Dozen-as well as a list of the fifteen kinds ofproduce that have the least amount of pesticide residue-the Clean Fifteen.

THE DIRTY DOZEN	
The 2016 Dirty Dozen includes the following produce. These are considered among the year's most important produce to buy organic:	
Strawberries	Spinach
Apples	Tomatoes
Nectarines	Bell peppers
Peaches	Cherry tomatoes
Celery	Cucumbers
Grapes	Kale/collard greens
Cherries	Hot peppers

The Dirty Dozen list contains two additional itemskale/collard greens and hot peppers-because they tend to contain trace levels of highly hazardous pesticides.

THE CLEAN FIFTEEN	
The least critical to buy organically are the Clean Fifteen list. The following are on the 2016 list:	
Avocados	Papayas
Corn	Kiw
Pineapples	Eggplant
Cabbage	Honeydew
Sweet peas	Grapefruit
Onions	Cantaloupe
Asparagus	Cauliflower
Mangos	

Some of the sweet corn sold in the United States are made from genetically engineered (GE) seedstock. Buy organic varieties of these crops to avoid GE produce.

Appendix 3 Index

JUDITH C. JONES

Printed in Great Britain
by Amazon

24020528R00053